SANTA FE'S
FONDA

The Story of the Old Inn at the End of the Trail

Allen R. Steele
Foreword by Rick Hendricks

Published by The History Press
Charleston, SC
www.historypress.com

Copyright © 2022 by Allen R. Steele
All rights reserved

Front cover, top left: photograph from the La Fonda Hotel archives; *top right*: Postcard in the La Fonda Hotel archives; *bottom*: Photograph from the La Fonda Hotel archives.
Back cover: author's collection; *insert*: photograph by T. Harmon Parkhurst, Wagon Train, New Mexico, 1925–1945, Courtesy of the Palace of the Governors Photo Archives (NMHM/DCA), negative Number 012014.

First published 2022

Manufactured in the United States

ISBN 9781467151153

Library of Congress Control Number: 2021950577

Notice: The information in this book is true and complete to the best of our knowledge. It is offered without guarantee on the part of the author or The History Press. The author and The History Press disclaim all liability in connection with the use of this book.

All rights reserved. No part of this book may be reproduced or transmitted in any form whatsoever without prior written permission from the publisher except in the case of brief quotations embodied in critical articles and reviews.

I am grateful to the management and staff of the La Fonda Hotel in Santa Fe for their cooperation and support of this endeavor to tell the story of their predecessor hotel that helped make the West. The staff of the hotel must be the most dedicated group to the maintenance and history of generous hospitality in the Southwest. If one includes both hotels that occupied the present site, this excellent hospitality has been offered for two hundred years! It has been one of the highlights of my life to associate with them in making the La Fonda a very special place in the annals of hostelry and warm hospitality in America.

When I proposed that I write a souvenir book about the old Exchange Hotel on the centennial anniversary of the La Fonda in 2022, the staff was anxious to be of help. That help went beyond moral support to opening the hotel archives and giving advice and support in the writing and planning of this book. Without their help and goodwill, it would have been a much weightier job to bring to life the stories of the old Exchange.

Because of my many wonderful years of association with the La Fonda, I wish to dedicate this volume to the hotel staff—past, present and future. May your determination to make visits to Santa Fe and the La Fonda memorable events in the lives of the thousands who visit the City Different and continue to distinguish the La Fonda as one of America's greatest homes away from home. May many weary travelers find life refreshed at the Inn at the End of the Trail.

CONTENTS

Foreword, by Rick Hendricks   7
Acknowledgements   9
Introduction   11

1. The Accidental Trailblazer   13
2. Three Pioneers   22
3. The Town at the End of the Trail   32
4. Permanent Arrivals   39
5. Turmoil in Santa Fe   48
6. Santa Fe Rebound   54
7. New Mexico Invaded   60
8. Santa Fe Booms   67
9. The Trail to California   75
10. Another Invasion   81
11. Prosperity   90
12. Incident at the Exchange   96
13. End of the Trail   101
14. A Festive Exchange   107
15. Resurrection   112
16. Still Standing   117
17. Santa Fe Style   124
18. A Hotel for the Making   129

Contents

Notes	133
Bibliography	147
Index	155
About the Author	159

FOREWORD

When visitors arrive in Santa Fe today from all over the world, they can choose from among a veritable profusion of accommodations when their day of seeing the sights is over. There are elegant hotels bedecked with rating stars where hospitality is king, very basic roadside lodgings and everything in between. Meals can range from the fabulously sumptuous to the merely filling. As Allen Steele clearly demonstrates in his lively history of the luxury hotel, La Fonda on the Plaza, this was not always the case. Early travelers in the Spanish period found no such welcome. If you were not someone of prominence, such as a civil-military official or a churchman, and you did not have kith or kin in Santa Fe, you were probably altogether out of luck.

In the Mexican period, which began in the 1820s and ended in the 1840s, as explorers, adventurers, merchants and an invading army came to New Mexico from the United States, the need for lodging grew. The plaza in the heart of Santa Fe was the western terminus of the Santa Fe Trail, and as people and products reached the end of their journey from Missouri, it was only logical that places to house the newcomers for a brief or extended stay would be established in that very spot.

Readers of this book will trek across the plains with William Becknell and Thomas James in those early years. Becknell is familiar to most folks with an interest in the Santa Fe Trail, but James is perhaps more important to the story of the development of hostelries in New Mexico's capital city. James rented a house from Francisco Ortiz, whom Steele refers to as the "Father of Santa Fe Hospitality." As the years went by, Ortiz and his neighbors rented

Foreword

properties at the corner of San Francisco Street and the Santa Fe Trail to foreigners from the States. Ortiz's property came to be known as the United States House.

By the 1840s, writers began to mention a guesthouse at that location. When such a place provided food as well as a place to sleep, it was called a *fonda* ("inn") in Spanish. The principal aim of this book is to trace the long history of La Fonda, in all its guises and through all its different names. It is just as much a history of a particular place at the end of a long human highway linking Missouri and New Mexico. In a much broader sense, the trail tied the Southwest to the rest of the United States to the east.

The author also traces the numerous changes in ownership of this special place through the years, providing a sort of genealogy of the venerable property. One can see the alterations to the structure and to the services the inn provided, which changed as proprietors came and went. There is, however, more here to learn about than just the history of La Fonda, interesting though that is. Because so many fascinating characters and important people stopped in at the hotel, telling the story of the building through the lives of the travelers who stayed there also neatly relates the history of Santa Fe through the second half of the nineteenth century. Moreover, there is a lot of history here of people who journeyed over the Santa Fe Trail and likely never darkened the doors of the inn at the end of the trail. Kit Carson puts in an appearance, as does Billy the Kid. Their stories and many others help fully illustrate the experiences of the travelers in those days, many of whom paused or ended their journey at the inn on the Plaza.

Most visitors to Santa Fe surely see La Fonda on the Plaza, constructed in Spanish–Pueblo revival style, and imagine that it is an ancient structure. They will doubtless be surprised to learn that the immediate forerunner of the current building—the Exchange Hotel—was razed in 1919. The architecture firm Rapp, Rapp, and Henderson was chosen to design La Fonda, and construction on the current iteration of the inn was completed in 1922.

Guests at La Fonda on the Plaza will enjoy learning in the pages of this book about the colorful history of the hotel and the lives of the countless fellow travelers who have tarried at the inn for a night's rest and a good meal in Santa Fe.

—Rick Hendricks, PhD
New Mexico State Records administrator

ACKNOWLEDGEMENTS

My sincere appreciation goes not only to the La Fonda Hotel family but also to many individuals who have helped along the way to make this book possible. The expert and prompt assistance at the Palace of the Governors was most helpful. The very obliging agreement by the Capitol Art Foundation for use of artwork in the book was encouraging. Among those who gave encouragement and support were Andrea Steele, Mimi Stewart, Jack Cloud, Elsie and Larry Davis, Steven Grover, David Torres, Rik Blythe, Ed Pulsifer, John Felix, Sita Jamison-Caddle, Raúl Burciaga, Catie Carl, Patricia Tapia, Patricia Palmer, Helen Pacheco, Rick Hendricks, Ben Gibson and Wenona Nutima.

INTRODUCTION

While it is tempting to think of New Mexico as the welcoming Land of Enchantment that it has become, this was not the case during its early Spanish centuries. In those days, freedom of travel was not a known thing. Only church or government officials and those pioneer colonists who accompanied them were granted free passage from village to village. All others were banned by law from entering the Spanish enclave. The entrance of foreigners—tourism as we know it today—was something that would not evolve until after the Spanish sway over the land diminished. Only after Mexican independence in 1821 were the natural beauties and cultural delights of the New Mexican experience open to visits by outsiders.

Many stories in the Spanish annals tell of intruders, few though they were, being locked up in Spanish *garitas*, or jails, where they would be tortured or languish for years until they died, unless they found some way to convince the officials that they should be set free. Zebulon Pike, the great American western explorer, nearly was imprisoned for his incursion into New Mexico in 1806, but the Spanish thought better of the idea when they realized they had an official U.S. representative on their hands. Fortunately for him, he was simply escorted back to U.S. territory.

Because of the strict ban by law of any individuals from America, France, England or other nations entering the vast territory during Spanish rule, the need for inns or hotels to house tourists was nonexistent. Traveling military officials of the Crown always knew they would find a bed at any military post on their journey. Traveling clergy always knew they could find shelter at the next church or mission station. Arriving Spanish colonists had to be self-supporting and carry their camp on their backs or in burro wagons until they found their own homestead. If a military base or church was not within a day's journey, large remote ranches owned by Spanish families had the burden of offering beds and breakfast.

Santa Fe, the capital founded in 1610, was the only city of any size in northern New Spain, and even there no inn could be found. When the Pueblo tribes revolted in 1680—the most successful Native American revolt in history—there were no records of an inn in the city. The Spanish, whether military or clergy, surely would have recorded such a facility had there been one, for they were the masters of detailed reports sent to headquarters. It is their meticulous reporting system that blesses us with infinite details about their wanderings and exploits during their time in the land. General Don Diego De Vargas, who came to oust the natives from the city after their twelve-year rule, reported that he found the city occupied only by government buildings and native-constructed houses, along with burned-out churches.

Then, in 1821, things changed. Mexico declared independence from Spain, and the new government, perhaps to its later regret, permitted open trade between the United States and Mexico. American-made manufactured goods were very welcome in the land that had previously relied on such items from distant Spain. American traders, who had been watching the momentum toward Mexican independence in the country south of the Rio Grande, jumped at the chance to risk the unknown and undeveloped trail—up to one thousand miles, depending on the starting point—across the Great Plains to the looming Rocky Mountains and the fabled city of Santa Fe. The first traders returned to their cash-strapped communities in Missouri as wealthy merchants.

As American trade with New Mexico escalated, the need for temporary housing for the newcomers became important. That's when several well-to-do Santa Fe families took advantage of the Americans' needs and started renting their domiciles to the extravagant merchants from the East. Then and there began the fascinating history of one of the nation's oldest hospitality corners, at the southwest corner of the ancient Santa Fe Plaza. The inn at the end of the Santa Fe Trail at San Francisco Street began the long history of hospitality in the West. This book records that fascinating history, based on the stories of the daring people who forged the way and pioneered hospitality in the American Southwest.

1

THE ACCIDENTAL TRAILBLAZER

The Prairies! The Wild Desert plains! After 15 days travel, here we are in a little paradise, a grove of tall trees, through which runs a beautiful stream of water over a pebble bottom. Flower and schrub [sic] in luxuriant profusion greet the eye and the cool breeze playing among the rustling leaves, adds variation to the songs of birds while the murmuring stream keeps up a running accompaniment.
—Matt Field, On the Santa Fe Trail, 3

The redheaded man sat at the kitchen table, his face in his hands. In his thirty-three years of life, he had been able to juggle business and finances deftly, but the current mess he found himself in was more than he could bear. What William Becknell worried about most of all was what he could do to save his family the humiliation of seeing him behind bars in a debtor's prison. He could hear the voices of his four children—two girls and twin boys, the oldest just six years old—as they played outside the house.

His wife, Mary, sent the children outdoors as soon as she sensed her husband's ugly mood. Now she sat quietly at his side. As he traced the mistakes over and over in his mind, he realized that it was time for fight or flight. He was known as a fighter, but now, at this precarious moment, he was facing a big decision: stay and face his mentors in Franklin, Missouri, or disappear for a while until the dust settled.

That was something he learned as a military man, a sergeant in the mounted militia under the command of Captain Nathan Boone, son of national hero Daniel Boone. As a battle-hardened soldier, he had learned that if the going gets tough, you either took your five-foot, eight-inch, 160-pound body into the fray, or (if you were smart enough to realize the overwhelming forces against you) you knew it was time to run if you wanted to live another day.[1]

Of immediate concern to his racking brain was the debt he had accumulated in deals with local landowners. Becknell owed approximately $1,000, and creditors were about to sue him to get their money back. In all his scrapes in life—and there had been quite a few—this was the deepest hole he had fallen into.[2]

Becknell was desperately searching for a way out of his dilemma. He had heard of people traveling west to the Spanish territory of New Mexico to trade, mostly with the Indian tribes that were numerous there. But the enterprise was dangerous. The Spanish did not welcome foreigners; they immediately put them in jail for trespassing. But maybe it was worth the risk.

The famous national story circulated about Zebulon Pike, sent in 1806 by the United States to reconnoiter the newly acquired Louisiana Territory. Pike passed through Missouri, traveled to the Rockies and was captured by Spanish dragoons at the Rio Grande. Escorted to Santa Fe, he was interviewed by the governor there then sent to Chihuahua for further interrogation. Fortunately, he and his team were not put in jail but were escorted back to the United States. They were government-sponsored, so they got off easy.[3]

Back in Franklin, the local newspaper, the *Missouri Intelligencer*, was reporting on the ongoing independence movement in Mexico. To Becknell, reading between the lines, it seemed that things would be changing rapidly as Spanish control waned in Mexico. Should he chance it?[4]

In 1819, an interesting entourage arrived at Franklin, led by Major Stephen Long. It was the Atkinson-Long, or Yellowstone, Expedition, another government-sponsored venture. Its mission was to travel by boat along the upper Missouri to find suitable sites for locating U.S. forts for defensive purposes. The mission halted for six days at Franklin, long enough for locals to learn every detail of the planned journey west. The expedition leaders gave lectures and shared their plans according to available maps, including Pike's drawings. This must have thrilled Becknell. He no doubt joined the throng of townspeople on the banks of the river for a rousing send-off when the Long team departed.[5]

Coinciding with these events, a land boom in America's West, especially in Missouri, brought many easterners out with the lure of cheap land, thanks to the U.S. government. Additionally, easy financial terms were offered. It would have been a great deal if the country had not also gone into debt along with its citizens. The purchase of the Louisiana Territory from France for $15 million put a strain on the U.S. treasury at a time when gold was in short supply. This critical situation resulted in the Panic of 1819, when creditors started demanding payment from their debtors, who had no money to give them.[6]

This was the very situation William Becknell found himself in. In an attempt to do something of value during desperate times, he ran for the U.S. House of Representatives, along with twenty-one other candidates, but he came up with only 431 votes, about half the number necessary to win. His disappointment in himself was compounded.[7] The idea of traveling west grew in his mind until it seemed like a vision from God Himself! By the spring of 1821, his decision had been made. Escaping Missouri and the creditors would be good for him, and he might strike gold in New Mexico. It was worth taking the chance.

On May 19, Joseph Cooper filed suit against him for the $321 owed him. Becknell had his attorney file a response in writing in July. The case would be reviewed by the court later that month. It would then be scheduled for trial—if Becknell was lucky, while he was away on the trip he was planning. With time running out, he had to work fast on his plan.

On June 25, he placed an ad in the *Missouri Intelligencer* seeking participants for a trip "to the westward for the purpose of trading for Horses & Mules, and catching Wild Animals of every description that we may think advantageous." Seventeen men responded to the call, and an organizational meeting was called for August 4 at the home of Ezekiel Williams. At the meeting, Becknell was unanimously elected captain of the enterprise. Two lieutenants were elected at a meeting on August 18. His organization, established along military lines, was ready. He also hired three Black slaves to serve the crew.[8]

A departure date of September 1 was set.[9] Becknell and his men met at the Arrow Rock crossing of the Missouri River near Franklin. He knew the place well, having acquired a license to operate the ferry there two years before.[10] They crossed to the southern side of the river with their packhorses and started the first leg of their trip by heading west along the south side of the great river.[11]

On the first day, they traveled six miles and then made camp. On the second day, they traveled thirty-three miles. With all the mental weight gone from planning and then launching the journey, Becknell was ebullient about the natural scenery: "The Petit Osage Plain…one of the most romantic and beautiful places in the state." The only thing that marred their movement was some rainstorms that made travel somewhat more challenging, because in the open plains, they had no place to shelter.

On the third night, the band reached Fort Osage, overlooking the Missouri River in Jackson County, Missouri, Becknell's last supply stop until Santa Fe. The fort, erected in 1808, consisted of a stockade built in a pentagonal form with two blockhouses placed at opposite angles. Inside were two series of buildings for soldiers' quarters and storehouses. It was on a high bluff with a commanding view of the river. Becknell says that at this remote outpost they "wrote letters, purchased some medicines and arranged such affairs as we thought necessary."

The wide and vast plains opened before them after leaving that last base of civilization. After crossing the wide and muddy Missouri again, a monotonous boredom began to settle in as they plodded westward. Becknell's only comment about this area tends to confirm this: "The country, for several days' travel from Fort Osage, is very handsomely situated, being high prairie, of exceeding fertility; but timber, unfortunately, is scarce."

By this time, they had crossed an area that in six years would turn into the town of Independence, the eventual jumping-off point for subsequent travelers on the Santa Fe Trail. It was at this spot that Lewis and Clark in 1803 stopped to pick plums, raspberries and wild apples on their way to Oregon. Becknell's group also crossed a line that fifty years later would become the Kansas state boundary. As they moved westward from the Missouri valley, the huge expanse of the Great Plains must have left them speechless, because Becknell left no description of this, a major part of their trip. It took them nearly two weeks to arrive at the Osage River, probably passing south of what would later become the cities of Lawrenceburg and Wichita.

The first noteworthy event from Becknell's journal comes when he became sick after chasing two elks they wounded in a hunt. They were unable to catch the animals, but he "was taken sick in consequence of heat and fatigue." Others in the company also suffered a malaise, "but determining not to surrender to trifles, or indulge in delay, until it became absolutely necessary, we continued to travel slowly."

Wildlife on the prairies was plentiful. They encountered buffalo, deer and wild goats. But heavy rain at times was bothersome, requiring that they stop to dry out their clothes and baggage. At twenty-four days out from Franklin, they came upon the Arkansas River. "The Arkansas at this place is about three hundred yards wide, very shallow, interrupted by bars and confined by

The Story of the Old Inn at the End of the Trail

A depiction of William Becknell on the Santa Fe Trail. *From a New Mexico State roadside historical marker.*

banks of entire sand," Becknell reported. The river water was too muddy for drinking, but they found a small stream flowing into the river that had "limpid and beautiful" water. They named it Hope Creek.

The travelers were surprised that they hadn't seen any Native Americans, especially as they were warned that these were the hunting grounds of the Plains tribes. "The absence of their company during our journey will not be a matter of regret," he wrote. In another day's travel, they crossed the Arkansas at a place where Becknell guessed the river was not more than eighteen inches deep and then camped on the other side.

The next day, they came upon a spectacle that the men had never seen before. Becknell gave quite a lot of space to this scene: a prairie dog town. He guessed the town covered ten acres! The men were entranced by the carrying-on of these little animals, their lookouts, their barks, their appearance and their interaction with humans. He killed one and tried to eat it after roasting. He found the meat "strong and unpalatable." They saw another animal "the size of a raccoon of a light grey color…fine fur, small eyes and…almost covered with shaggy hair." They also caught a large rabbit that they figured was about the size of a Missouri fox.

On their twenty-fifth day out from Franklin, they camped at the edge of a sea of sand dunes, where they endured a torrential downpour until the next morning. They were becoming dependent on the buffalo that were so abundant; they used dried buffalo manure to make a fire over which they cooked buffalo meat for breakfast. "So far as the eye can reach, on every side, the country here appears alive with buffalo and other animals," he said. The study of these animals intrigued Becknell. He observed firsthand an attack on the big animals by a pack of wolves. When planning an attack, "a company of from ten to twenty divide into two parties, one of which separates a buffalo from the herd, and pursues him."

By one o'clock the next day, they came upon the salt flats of the Arkansas River, a few miles southeast of the future Dodge City. They then followed the meandering river. Becknell reported that a number in the party were suffering from "ill health," probably due to the drenching rain, poor food and exhaustion. At the same time, their horses were tiring of the grueling travel and tried to bolt from the camp; one succeeded and was never seen again. The horses were so weak the men decided to take a three-day break in travel so the animals could recover. It also gave the men some time to fashion moccasins for themselves.

They were now in what Becknell called "high prairie" and found rattlesnakes galore living in holes in the ground along the riverbank. On September 21, they came to some forks of the river and followed a tributary south, probably the river later named the Pergatoire. It was here that they first became aware that they were not alone on the prairies: they heard a gunshot in the distance and assumed it was from a Native American hunter, but they saw no more evidence of his presence.

With mountains arising in the distance, they followed that river to its source, where they faced the daunting task of finding a way across a steep mountain. The mountainside was so rocky it took them two days to clear a passageway to gain access to the other side. It is surmised they crossed at Emery Gap, not far from the Raton Pass.[12] They lost another horse in the process but in the end finished up the month on the other side and in sight of more rolling plains. Becknell seemed to think this was their lowest point in morale and fatigue. He noted that they had been traveling fifty days and "our diet being altogether different…and unexpected hardships and obstacles occurring almost daily, our company is much discouraged." They were only making eight to fifteen miles each day, and they experienced their first snow shower.

Two days on the other side of the mountain, they came upon the rugged cliffs of the Canadian River or one of its tributaries. They found it a tricky river to cross because of sandbars and quicksand. They had to camp one night without a fire due to lack of wood. But as they continued south, suddenly their fortunes began to change. They found the country more level and pleasant, and they began to see small herds of wild horses. There was also evidence of sheep herding. And traveling south by December 12 they actually came to a trail that led them through patches of pine and cottonwood trees. "The prospect of a near termination of our journey excites hope and redoubled exertion." The signs of human activity were obviously very encouraging.

And then the biggest surprise of the journey happened. On the morning of November 13, a party of Spanish troops was seen heading their way! Any anxiety the Americans might have had at seeing the soldiers approach was soon forgotten, as, on greeting, the soldiers actually seemed very friendly. Although they spoke no English, their smiling faces and otherwise goodwill seemed a miracle to the Americans. Becknell soon learned that the army contingent was under the command of Captain Don Pedro Ignacio Gallego. The captain was under orders from the governor of New Mexico, Facundo

A section of the Pecos River at San Miguel del Vado, where the ford of the river signaled entry into Mexican territory. *Author's collection.*

Melgares, in Santa Fe. The Mexican force, it was revealed, was searching the area for a trace of marauding Indians who had raided a town to the south. The Americans felt compelled to trust the Spaniards' friendliness sufficiently to camp with them that night.[13]

Gallego identified the place of their meeting as the Puertocito de la Piedra Lumbre. It was a wilderness place located just south of the future Las Vegas, New Mexico. Gallego said he "Parlayed" with Becknell that afternoon, even though he admitted he could not understand English and Becknell could not understand Spanish. The Spanish leader finally decided the best course of action would be to lead the Americans to the next logical stop on the way to Santa Fe.[14]

The dragoons led them to the first Spanish village the Americans had ever seen, San Miguel del Vado, where they were welcomed heartily. The importance of this town, they discovered, was that it was at a ford of the Pecos River. Also important was the presence of a certain Frenchman. "Fortunately, I here met with a Frenchman, whose language I imperfectly understand, and hired him to proceed with us to Santa Fe, in the capacity of an interpreter," said Becknell.

Ancient adobe walls of building ruins at San Miguel del Vado village. *Author's collection.*

The Story of the Old Inn at the End of the Trail

After a night in San Miguel, the Americans set out early, headed east. The Mexican militia set out after them at 6:00 a.m. with the intention of escorting them into Santa Fe. However, in the process, it seems they decided to turn north in pursuit of the Native Americans they were sent to find. Gallego's diary records that they headed along the eastern side of the mountains into the vicinity of the village of Taos, well north of Santa Fe.

Both parties passed by the ruins of the great Pecos Pueblo, the town overlooking the river valley. The vast ruins at Pecos testified to its one-time importance as the ancient trade center between the Pueblos and the Plains tribes. Two days out from San Miguel del Vado, and after crossing mountain country at the southern end of the Rockies, the team came upon a downward slope into the fabled city of Santa Fe. In unbelief, they passed through the Barrio de Analco, past San Miguel Chapel and forded the Santa Fe River, nodding at pedestrians who stopped to wave their welcome to the strangers. Becknell summed it up: "We were received with apparent pleasure and joy."

It was November 16, 1821. They had traveled about one thousand miles in seventy-seven days.

2
THREE PIONEERS

The "Arkansaw" [sic] in the noon-day beam
Is a beautiful and grassy stream
With its Buffalo herds on its banks of green,
And its fairy-like Islands that live between,
Is a sight, in the sun or the moonlight sheen
Lovely and beautiful to be seen.
—*Matt Field,* On the Santa Fe Trail, *28–29*

As leader of his team, William Becknell, the first successful American trader to freely enter, sell goods and freely depart Santa Fe, is crowned by historians as the "Father of the Santa Fe Trail." His claim to that title, if he ever learned that he had such a title, was confirmed when he took wagons along the trail on his second trip in 1822. Another trader, a Missourian, might be worthy of the name "Father of the River Trail to Santa Fe," for by following the Arkansas River most of the way cross-country, he arrived at Santa Fe on December 1, barely two weeks after Becknell. He was Thomas James, of St. Louis. While both men were en route to Santa Fe, newspapers in Missouri were reporting details of Mexico's independence that culminated with the Treaty of Cordoba on September 27.[15]

Becknell sold all of his merchandise in a month and left Santa Fe on December 13. His investment of $300 in trade goods brought in a $6,000 return, more than enough to square away his debts back in Missouri. He made the trip again in 1822 with $3,000 worth of goods in three wagons and returned home with a profit of $91,000. Back in Missouri, he went on to become a justice of the peace. Then, in 1828, he was elected to the House of Representatives in the state legislature. In 1835, he sold all he had in Missouri and moved to Red River County in Texas. There he took part in the Texas Revolution and later served in the Texas Rangers. He died on April 25, 1856, as a major landowner and was buried near Clarksville.[16]

James, however, unlike Becknell, stayed on in Santa Fe for several months, until June 1822. His reason for heading to Santa Fe was similar to Becknell's: as a merchant in his city, he "struggled on through the years of 1819–20, with the certain prospect of bankruptcy before my face, amid the clamors of creditors, and without the hope of extricating myself from impending ruin," he said. During the time of his deepest financial woes, several American men with an incredible story arrived in St. Louis. They were recently returned from prison in Chihuahua, jailed there ten years simply for entering Spanish territory. They were "the first American Santa Fe Traders that carried goods from St. Louis to New Mexico," James claimed, and they were jailed for their efforts.[17]

With the expected independence of Mexico, James decided to head west. His cross-country trip involved much more human interaction with Native Americans than did Becknell's. He set a course for Santa Fe by way of the Arkansas River from its mouth on the Mississippi, inland until he should arrive in the area of New Mexico. "I loaded a keel-boat with goods to the value of $10,000 and laid in a large quantity of biscuit, whiskey, flour, lead and powder, for trading with the Indians on the route," he said. He left St. Louis on May 10, 1821, and headed down the Mississippi to where the Arkansas joined the big river, about one hundred miles south of the upstart town of Memphis.

James says he had heard that "all the Indians on our route were friendly," although he didn't say how he acquired the information. The Arkansas flowed through the old capital of the Arkansas Territory, Eau Post, and on to the new capital, Little Rock. He passed safely through the lands of the Quapaw, Cherokee and Osage. Near a place where the future Tulsa, Oklahoma, would be settled, the river became too shallow to continue by boat. He abandoned the boat and bought twenty-three horses from the Osage tribe and transferred his goods onto the backs of the animals.[18]

Soon after they set out again, they became aware that they were being followed. The next morning, they were greeted by about one hundred Comanche, who demanded gifts. James and three of his men were then

A view of the Arkansas River in Colorado. The river was a waymark and a source of water for those who traveled the Santa Fe Trail. *Author's collection*.

compelled to visit the Indian village, where more gifts were demanded and their horses taken. He said, "The Indians began to gather around us, and break open and drag about the goods." He feared he would lose all his cargo and maybe his life. "Our time seemed nearly come," he said.

After three days of threats by the Native Americans and sleepless nights, their end seemed near when all of a sudden a cry went up from the malevolent warriors, "Tabbaho, Tabbaho. White men." At the sound of hoofbeats, James looked to the southwest and "saw six horsemen riding at full speed, and as they came nearer, we heard the words in Spanish, 'save them, save them.' In a moment a Spanish officer rushed into our arms, exclaiming, 'Thank God we are in time.'" The officer explained that he had heard of their plight that morning and rode twenty miles to save them.

"He asked the Indians why they were going to kill us. They answered that the Spanish governor in Santa Fe had commanded them not to let any American pass…they thought they were compelled to take our lives." This is when James first heard about the reality of an independent Mexico. Addressing the Indians, the officer "told them that this was under the government of Spain, but that they were now independent and free, and brothers to the Americans." The traders then mounted up to ride with the Spanish contingent to their camp.

At the camp, they were met by an imposing figure, "a tall Indian of about seventy years of age, dressed in the complete regimentals of an American Colonel, with blue coat, red sash, white pantaloons, epaulets and sword." He was Chief Cordaro. He saluted and handed James a piece of paper. It read:

> *This is to certify that Cordaro, a Chief of the Comanches has visited the Fort at Nacotoche with fifteen of his tribe, that he remained here two weeks, and during the whole time behaved very well. It is my request that all Americans who meet him or any of his tribe, should treat him and them with great respect and kindness, as they are true friends of the United States.*
> —*John Jameson, U.S. Indian Agent at Nacotoche on Red River*

Chief Cordaro "was the cause of our being then in existence. He told us he had promised his 'great friend at Nacotoche' that he would protect all Americans that came through his country, and he very earnestly requested us to inform his 'great friend' that he had been as good as his word." James then said, "Cordaro…appeared to rejoice at our escape as much as we."

After a farewell to the soldiers, the traders continued their trek west following the banks of the Canadian River. Within three days, they were in

Ruins of the Spanish Mission Church, built in 1717 at Pecos. Thomas James stayed the night at this spot at the end of his first day of travel in Mexican territory. *The La Fonda Hotel Archives.*

sight of the snow-capped Rocky Mountains, the Sangre de Cristo Range. At the sight of the mountains, they knew they should head south to reach the mountain pass into Santa Fe. In five more days, they arrived at San Miguel del Vado to cross the Pecos River at the same spot Becknell had done not too many days before. Fifteen miles out from San Miguel, they reached the Pueblo village of Pecos.

James's detailed description of Pecos provides an idea of the grandness of this, the most eastern of the Pueblo Indian villages and the place where trade fairs between the Pueblos and the Plains Indians were held. "I slept in the fort which encloses two or three acres in an oblong, the sides of which are bounded by brick houses three stories high without any entrances in front....A balcony surmounted the first and second stories and moveable ladders were used in ascending to them." He noticed heaps of rocks on the houses' flat roofs, kept "for annoying an enemy." He was told "this town and Fort are of unknown antiquity, and stood there in considerable splendor in the time of the Conquerors." Unfortunately, within a few years, the townspeople vacated Pecos, and it soon became a ghost town.

Remnants of village walls at Pecos. The village was an important landmark on the Santa Fe Trail just a short journey from Santa Fe. *Author's collection*.

On the evening of the next day, they arrived at Santa Fe. "The houses were all white-washed outside and in, and presented a very neat and pleasing sight to the eye of the traveler. They are all flat on the roof." In contrast, he reported that there were five Roman Catholic churches that towered above the houses. In this Spanish-speaking town, he was fortunate to obtain the services of Alcalde Don Francisco Ortiz to translate and from whom he rented a house.[19]

The next day, James was introduced to Governor Melgares, who gave him permission to begin selling his goods in the city. "After about six weeks… my true friend and protector, Cordaro, came in…with thirty of his tribe to ascertain if we were at liberty." He then spoke to a council of city leaders

Santa Fe's Fonda

and admonished them that the Americans now, with Mexican independence assured, were friends. After the meeting, Cordaro asked James to write the letter he had requested for Colonel Jameson at Nacatoche. "I wrote the letter and delivered it to him. On the next day we parted and I never saw him again." James later found out, on a subsequent journey to Santa Fe, that the old chief had, indeed, gone to Nacatoche, showed the letter to the officials there and was given three horses loaded with gifts. He then went back to his country "a rich man, and soon after became sick and died."

According to James, trading was not very profitable for him in Santa Fe, "on account of the scarcity of money." However, he was soon to contribute something of great value to the populace. February 5 was set for a celebration of Mexican Independence in the town square, the Plaza. By this time, instructions had been distributed to all Mexican territories in the country as to how the new Mexico was to be organized and governed. The information was printed in the *Gaceta Imperial Estraordinaria de Mexico*. New Mexico was identified as a valid department of the empire with representation in the national Regency. But the Spanish had ruled for over two hundred years, and local officials were not sure how to celebrate.[20]

The Palace of the Governors on the Santa Fe Plaza, where Governor Malgares welcomed the first American merchants to New Mexico, William Becknell and Thomas James. *Postcard in the La Fonda Hotel archives.*

James came to the rescue. A meeting was held in the alcalde's house to plan the event. James was handy, and "they sent for me, asked what was the custom in my country on such occasions, and requested my advice." He recommended the raising of a flag and asked what was the national emblem and motto to be on the flag. As of that time, they did not know of any. "I recommended the Eagle, but they at last agreed upon two clasped hands in sign of brotherhood and amity with all nations."

The morning of the celebration arrived. James went to the Plaza to help supervise. He informed the governor that as head of state, he should take the honor of raising the flag. "'Oh do it yourself,' said he, you understand such things. So I raised the first flag in the free and independent State of New Mexico." As the flag was raised, canons fired and the commotion caught the attention of everyone in town. Soon the Plaza was filled with people from town and country. The festivities lasted five days.

James continued on in the city for a few more months, but because trading there was not profitable, he asked Ortiz for advice. His friend suggested that he go to Sonora on the Gulf of California, with a member of the Ortiz family to accompany him. But Ortiz later warned him that he should obtain permission from the governor to leave Santa Fe. The governor at first refused to permit him to go. James insisted that he had every right to make the trip; besides, his friend Don Francisco Ortiz was willing to send his son of the same name as his guide. The governor ridiculed his plan. Realizing the trip was probably not going to happen, James decided to go to Taos, north of Santa Fe, the fur-trading center, and from there head back across the plains to Missouri.

On the first of June, he "bade adieu forever to the capital of New Mexico, and was perfectly content, never to repeat my visit to it or any other part of the country." He returned to St. Louis and to all his debts. He estimated he lost $12,000 on his Santa Fe adventure but eventually recovered his losses. He was forced to sell everything he owned, and he moved across the Mississippi into Illinois, just opposite St. Louis. In 1825, he was elected general of the Second Brigade, First Division of the Militia of Illinois and became a member of the Illinois legislature for two terms. His last stint in government service was as postmaster in Monroe County.

To General Thomas James we owe much of what we know about Santa Fe in the early 1820s. The fabled city, officially named by the Spanish "The Royal City of the Holy Faith of St. Francis of Assisi" in 1610, was well over two hundred years old when Becknell and James arrived in 1821. A main street, San Francisco Street, was named after the same saint as the city. About midway on this street was a central square, the Plaza, with public and private buildings on all four sides. On the north side of the square was the Palace of the Governors, the seat of government for the whole of New Mexico. From the four corners of the square roads reached out in different directions, for this was the crossroads of the Southwest.[21]

A road going north led to the towns of Cieneguilla, Picuris and Taos. In the northwest corner of the Plaza, a road became a route to the Rio Grande, the town of Abiquiu and west to Utah and California. The most important road started at the southwest corner of the Plaza; it was the Camino Real, the Royal Road, and continued south to a village called Albuquerque and on to Socorro, El Paso, Chihuahua and Mexico City. For centuries, it was the lifeline of the city; over it caravans brought cargo to supply the shops, government and churches from the capital of New Spain, Mexico City.

Becknell's and James's entry point at the southeast corner of the Plaza was probably of least importance to the Spanish authorities in the 1800s. That road led east to the ancient trade center, Pecos, and to San Miguel del Vado. From there, trails formed for centuries by human feet and, when the Spanish arrived, by horses' hooves, led in all directions across the Great Plains of the continent's Midwest. Native Americans traveled those trails from time immemorial, but ruling Europeans had little need for them, because their interests lay to the south, west and north, to interior population centers.

The Europeans were limited by the bounds of the Spanish Empire, and the plains to their east were seen as distant, desolate and uninhabitable. There were occasions when marauding bands of Comanche, Kiowa or other Plains tribes dared to cross the mountains into the Rio Grande Valley. Then the Spanish-organized cabals would take the trail past Pecos and San Miguel del Vado and out to the plains to punish the retreating invaders.

For centuries, travelers who entered the city found overnight accommodation according to their status or type of business. Clerics could be assured of a good night's sleep in guest rooms maintained by the church. Civil servants could plan on having a bed in a government guesthouse. Military personnel could stay at a military post. Foreigners, of which there were almost none, were obliged to find accommodation wherever they could. Fortunately, the Native American and Spanish people were very hospitable and welcomed the chance to host a visitor in their dwelling, be it large or small.

Zebulon Pike, while in Santa Fe in 1807 to be interviewed by the governor, stayed in the home of a Mr. Bartholemé, someone he called his friend and most likely the man who would become governor some years later. Apparently, there were not many choices for accommodation in Santa Fe at that time, and the best arrangement was in the home of a local. This was better than the alternative, the *garita*. The jail was a fixture in Spanish cities. Santa Fe's garita was located on the north side of town, near where the U.S. Army would later build a military fortress called Fort Marcy. The garita was where enemies of the Crown were imprisoned and executed.[22]

Thomas James's ability to rent a house from Don Francisco Ortiz was not only fortunate for him but was also convenient, located as it was on the new trail coming into the Plaza from the east. It was probably one of the finest houses Thomas saw as he came into the town proper. Not only that, but the owner, Ortiz, was also the city alcalde, chief magistrate. With this connection, James was in a position to receive all the courtesies of an honored guest.[23]

Ortiz could easily be considered "Father of Santa Fe Hospitality," one among the triumvirate Santa Fe Trail pioneers, with Becknell and Thomas. As he welcomed visitors from the east and rented his house to these new American visitors, he unknowingly started what was to become the American rental district of Santa Fe. His house and four others on the corner of the Old Santa Fe Trail and San Francisco Street were also at the start of one of the Southwest's most famous hospitality properties.[24]

His example of welcoming visitors from the east as they came into Santa Fe, usually tired, dirty and hungry, started a tradition that would continue for hundreds of years. He would live to see the property turn into the town's first multiroom inn and eatery.

3
THE TOWN AT THE END OF THE TRAIL

Bricks moulded [sic] *from prairie clay*
And roasted in the noontide ray
Large as the stones of city halls
Form good...strong built walls
And trunks and boughs of "Cotton Wood"
Form gates and beams and rafters good.
—Matt Field, On the Santa Fe Trail, *44*

With spreading knowledge of the successful trips of Becknell and Thomas. a flow of visitors began arriving from the United States that would swell into the thousands in a few years' time. As far as can be determined, Don Francisco Ortiz and his neighbors at the corner of San Francisco Street and the Santa Fe Trail continued to rent out rooms, or entire houses, to the increasing stream of traders from the east. It became known by traders that this is where you could rent a house to live comfortably and also display your wares for sale. So much so that, soon, the Ortiz house became known as the *Los Estados Unidos*—or "The United States"—house.[25]

In 1822, Becknell returned to trade in Santa Fe with a team of twenty-five men, twenty-eight horses and three wagons. In the process, at one point, their horses were stolen by the Osage Indians and later retrieved. When they finally had the village of San Miguel in sight, they fired their guns in salute and received a warm welcome. Becknell's review of the trip caused him to remark that trade at Santa Fe was "very profitable, money and mules are plenty and they do not hesitate to pay the price demanded." He added about the trail, "A few places would require much labor to render them passable." But "a road might be...laid out," and this would bring him to the attention of government leaders in Missouri. He was later invited to help further develop the trail.[26]

Shortly after Becknell, then Thomas, left the city, local government was organized according to decrees from Mexico City. Santa Fe was now permitted to be governed by a representative form of government. Governor Melgares, who had interviewed Becknell and James, was now in his new capacity of *jefe politico*, or political chief. He organized the formation of primary elections of *electores* to represent fourteen alcaldes, or districts, of the territory according to Mexico's new policies. Naturally, members of the privileged class of New Mexican society were elected and met in Santa Fe for the first time.[27]

By early 1823, Bartolomé Baca was elected governor. He realized the potential for Santa Fe to become a profitable transshipment point between the United States and Mexico's interior provinces and decided to see if riches could be made the other way around, Santa Fe to Missouri. In the spring of 1824, the governor sent word to Major O'Fallon at Fort Atkinson in Council Bluffs that he could expect him to arrive with a trade caravan on or about June 10. He also wanted to put on a show of strength to the tribes along the way that were hampering both Mexican and American traders. His trip was deemed successful and added importance to Santa Fe as the major transshipment center for American trade with Chihuahua and points south.[28]

The traders from the east arrived in increasing numbers, from twenty-six wagons in 1824, increasing to one hundred wagons in 1828. The value of goods increased from $35,000 in 1824 to $150,000 in 1828. In that latter year, $20,000 worth of goods was transshipped to Chihuahua. By the 1840s, the major portion of traders was New Mexicans, securing goods from the east and transporting them to Santa Fe.[29]

With the widening fame of Santa Fe as the West's main trading center, the city came under close scrutiny from those who anxiously arrived after such long sojourns across the prairies. It also became a favorite topic for people in the United States who nurtured curiosity about this fabled town newly opened to the rest of the world. Descriptions of the New Mexican capital city appeared in journals across the country.

Becknell, writing for his hometown newspaper about his visit, gave his first impression by sharing that it was "in a valley of the mountains...about

A wagon train on the Santa Fe Trail. *Photograph by T. Harmon Parkhurst, Wagon Train, New Mexico, 1925–1945, Courtesy of the Palace of the Governors Photo Archives (NMHM/DCA), negative Number 012014.*

two miles long and one mile wide…compactly settled." He reported, "The walls of their houses are two or three feet thick, built of…brick and are uniformly one story high, having a flat roof made of clay." He also noted the sparseness of furniture inside the homes, as "they do not know the use of plank and have neither chairs nor tables." His description of home interiors seems to imply that he stayed in a house during his visit rather than having to endure an outdoor camping situation.[30]

James gives some added information. As he entered the city, "It presented a fine appearance…It is beautifully situated on a plain of dry and rolling ground, at the foot of a high mountain, and a small stream…runs directly through the city." He estimated the population to be six thousand. "The houses are all flat on the roof." He noted the city had five churches and the "principal buildings are built around the public square in the middle of the city." As for agriculture, both men noticed various table crops being cultivated, but the unusually large size of onions grown there surprised both men. James added that he saw red peppers being cultivated, "a principal ingredient in Spanish food."

Ten years after Becknell and James entered Santa Fe, another Missourian, Josiah Gregg, decided to head west. His motivation was finding a health-seeking climate—he was suffering from tuberculosis. His doctor did

The Story of the Old Inn at the End of the Trail

As travelers on the Santa Fe Trail entered Santa Fe, the first building of note they would have seen as they entered the Barrio de Analco, the oldest neighborhood in the city, was San Miguel Chapel. *Author's collection*.

everything he could for his ailment. But eventually, when there was nothing more that would help his weakened condition, Gregg was advised to take a trip west. He gave his own description of the city: "The town is irregularly laid out.…The only attempt at anything like architectural…compactness consists of four tiers of buildings, whose fronts are shaded with a fringe of portales [porches]…of the rudest possible description.…They stand around the public square."[31]

Another visitor in 1839 recalled his entrance into the city. "There, within half a mile of the base of the mountain, a small spot of the vast green plain…was dotted with low one-story buildings, reminding us irresistibly of an assemblage of mole hills." Matt Field, an actor from St. Louis, also headed west to improve his health. "The apartments are of various lengths but never exceeding twenty feet in width…as all the dwellings are connected it is not uncommon to see children chasing each other the whole length of a street along the house tops." Field mentions the practice of traders to rent accommodations near the central square.[32]

Since no one writing before 1833 mentions the existence of a hotel or guesthouse, we can only assume there was none. Certainly, if there were, it would have been included as a major establishment near the town square. Inevitably, travelers who visit a new place will mention the hotel where they stayed, but here, only the rental of a house was mentioned. All of the people who wrote about the city at that time say only that, other than government buildings and churches, there were only private homes.

But that was about to change, because within ten years, writers of the time began mentioning the existence of a one-story guesthouse at the corner of San Francisco Street and the Santa Fe Trail. In time, the houses on that site were gradually combined and transformed into an inn to accommodate the increasing numbers of people arriving from the East. Locals began to call it the "inn"—or "fonda," if you spoke Spanish.

Most city houses with their courtyards lent themselves to easy transition to a larger accommodation. What's more, individual rooms in New Mexican homes, while interconnected by interior doorways, were accessed from the courtyard and could easily be turned into private rooms. Extant records are absent that would tell us how that happened or who did it, nevertheless, our imagination leads us to conclude that that was what happened. We can suggest that the transformation was at the instigation of Don Francisco Ortiz and his fellow property owners as they saw the need arise.[33]

These plans for added hospitality came none too soon. On April 1, 1924, a group of fifty men met to organize the largest wagon train yet to head out for Santa Fe. Like Becknell, they met to organize in Franklin. Among the group were two men who were destined to become influential in western expansion: M.M. Marmaduke, who would later become governor of Missouri; and Augustus Storrs, who, in 1925, was appointed U.S. consul to Santa Fe. The trip via the Santa Fe Trail would be not only exciting for them but also very educational.

The twenty-five wagons set out on May 15 and arrived in Santa Fe on July 28. After their trip of four months and ten days, the party returned to Franklin triumphantly with $180,000 in gold and silver and $10,000 worth of furs. It turned out to be one of the most successful trade ventures in the nearly sixty-year history of the trail.[34]

Huge profits continued to be made in the trade ventures, even after new governor Baca announced in late 1824 that the duty on imports would rise to 50 percent. The flood had started, and it would grow, from wagons loaded with merchandise to wagons loaded with pioneers heading west in search of a new life. The effect on Santa Fe was profound. It would cease being a closed and distant city; the trade would enliven its commerce and social life.

Routine daily life in the city would carry on until it was known that a wagon train was on the way. Matt Field described the excitement of a wagon train's arrival: "The arrival of...a caravan from the States is, both to the natives and transient residents, an affair of much enlivening interest." He said somehow the nearing of a wagon train was usually known up to ten days before it actually reached the city, and during "this interim is all occupied in anticipation, curiosity, and speculation." The event heralded the import of new merchandise and incoming mail and news from the United States, and "The *Senoritas* who figure at *fandangos*, look for new faces...while the customhouse officers grow more important in their bearing, and are constantly on the alert, ready for the jealous scrutiny of the newcomers."

Excitement grew intense as the cavalcade entered the town proper and "whips were heard cracking round a distant corner." The mule and oxen drivers tried to outdo each other with all the noise and commotion they could create, especially the cracking of whips and yells at the patient animals that had brought them to the end of the trail. "On they came up the street, and old and young, American and Mexican, all sorts and sexes, assembled at the doors and windows and in the street, to witness the procession."

The wagons were then unloaded for customs inspection and taken away to be parked, and the animals were turned out to pasture "to rest and feast for six long months, and evening scarcely darkened over the town before the pass whiskey began to operate, and groups of noisy American drivers were heard singing, shouting, and rioting in every street." Then musicians with fiddles and guitars would appear to start the evening dance, known as the fandango. These dance parties would usually continue without abandon through most of the night.[35]

4
PERMANENT ARRIVALS

Our attention was attracted…by the appearance of some three or four objects in motion at a great distance away.…We continued on our way with our eyes fixed upon the far horizon where these objects were seen. It was soon evident that what we saw could not be buffalo, and a very few moments more brought us to the conviction that a band of wild horses was approaching.…Suddenly…he shouted…Comanches! Comanches!
—*Matt Field,* On the Santa Fe Trail, *265*

The teenage boy with curling reddish hair bent over the huge leather hide on the table before him. It was his job to trace and cut out as many segments from each swath of saddle leather as possible, according to a pattern given him by the saddlemaker. His boss demanded that any amount of waste of the cowhide was too much waste, and he would check to make sure this stringent rule was followed. Christopher, the sixth of ten siblings, had taken on this apprenticeship rather than try to deal with the chaos at home. It was his job to repeat the same routine every day: open up the shop, light a fire in the fireplace, sharpen knives and awls and head for a day at the cutting table.

The Carson family, originally from Kentucky, now, in 1825, lived in Franklin, Missouri. Christopher was called "Kit" by his family, and it was a nickname that would follow him the rest of his life. He could abide his nine brothers and sisters if he had to, but his stepfather was intolerable. Even though it had been his decision to apprentice with the saddlemaker, he hated the tedious and monotonous job.

Santa Fe's Fonda

Anxious to escape his captivity, he began planning a breakout. He would go west, like Lewis and Clark, Pike and Becknell. The next year, a wagon train was forming in town, and he determined to be on it. As preparations accelerated for the big event, Kit secretly sought out the wagon master, Charles Bent, businessman and trader. Bent asked him what he could do that would make him valuable to his employer. "I can shoot straight," replied the boy. He was signed on as "cavvy," caretaker of the animals, which would make the journey possible.

Early on the day of departure, Kit, the poor, illiterate sixteen-year-old, did not appear at the saddle shop. He was on his way west with the wagon train. Asked why he left his job, he said his boss "was a good man....But taking into consideration that if I remained with him...I would have to pass my life in labor that was distasteful to me." But more than that, "being anxious to travel for the purpose of seeing different countries, I concluded to join the first party that started for the Rocky Mountains."[36]

In some weeks, the wagon train arrived in Santa Fe. Kit Carson got his first glimpses of the capital city as he toured the town for a couple days. He then went north seventy miles to Taos, where he spent the winter of 1826–27 at the house of a retired mountaineer. It was in Taos that he learned Spanish. From French trappers he learned French, and it was reported that he learned eight or nine tribal languages. Kit decided Taos was his kind of town.

Charles Bent and his brother William also traveled north, back up to the Arkansas River, where they built a trading center, actually a fortress, to take advantage of the Santa Fe and Indian trade. The center was called "Bent's Fort." Kit would have been amazed if someone at this point had suggested that he and Charles would one day become brothers-in-law, but that's what happened when Kit married his third wife who was sister to Bent's wife! He would have been shocked if anyone told him that the same man's life would end with two bullets to his chest. The Bents and Carson would become fellow defenders of the commerce of the prairies for years to come. And both names would become synonymous with that of Santa Fe.

The young Kit Carson was the epitome of thousands of young men who came west to stay and call it home. Adventure called them. Hunting and trapping in the Rocky Mountains was profitable and exciting. That in itself was a challenge for society in the territory: American white women were nowhere to be found. Native American girls and Spanish *señoritas* soon became wives of these mountain men, who found Taos to be a good base for operations and family making.

But in Santa Fe, the traders came to stay for only a short time and then headed back home. These visitors, the merchants, were transient; temporary accommodations for them were in short supply. And the hospitable residents of the town were not yet tuned into what an overnight stay should look like for these merchantmen from the capitalistic East. An eastern woman's touch was needed.

Enter Mary Donoho, reportedly the first white American woman to travel the Santa Fe Trail. She would become known as the fourth pioneer of the Santa Fe Trail and begin a legacy for women who would follow in creating one of America's most iconic hospitality traditions, at the *fonda*, the Inn at the End of the Trail.

General Kit Carson, circa 1880–1900. *Courtesy of the Palace of the Governors Photo Archives (NMHM/DCA), negative Number 007152.*

Mary Dodson was born in Tennessee in 1807. She was one of ten children to Dr. and Mrs. James Dodson, who moved to Missouri in the late 1820s. William Donoho, her future husband, was born in Kentucky in 1798 but moved to Boone County, Missouri, in the late 1820s. That's where the two young people met. William and Mary married in Columbia, Missouri, on November 27, 1831.[37]

Obviously, William became aware of the incredible returns for Missouri merchants who were involved in the Santa Fe trade and decided to try his hand at the same. Whether his wife had the same enthusiasm for the idea or not is not clear. Nevertheless, their travel adventure west took place in the summer of 1833. The experienced Charles Bent was elected leader of the caravan, and all parties were ordered to join at Council Grove on the Santa Fe Trail in the Kansas Territory. Heavy rains caused arrival delays. But the Donohos, including their first daughter, Mary Ann, were among the travelers.

A Ranger battalion from Fort Leavenworth under the command of Captain William N. Wickliffe was sent to protect them through the U.S. territory portion of the trip. He had 150 men in his contingent. Soon, the men of the battalion were underway. The journey was without incident right up to the Arkansas crossing, where the trail turned sharply south toward the New Mexico border. Here the military escort officially completed its assignment and turned to head back to Missouri, leaving the caravan on its own to complete the journey.[38]

A well-worn section of the Santa Fe Trail in northern New Mexico. *Author's collection.*

The parade ground in Bent's Old Fort at La Junta, Colorado. *Author's collection.*

Once the unguarded caravan got well into Mexican territory, they found they were constantly being followed by Indians on all sides. One sortie by the natives was thwarted by the traders who went out to deal with them on horseback. "When at a about the distance of a hundred yards they fled and never afterward approached nearer than a mile," reported Richard B. Lee, a furloughed army officer with the caravan. "We reached our destination without an adventure although we passed within fifteen or twenty miles of an encampment of several thousand Comanche and Kiowa Indians."[39]

A good assumption is that on arrival at Santa Fe in August 1833, William did what traders did before him: he rented a house, or two adjacent houses, where his family could live and his wares could be put on display for sale. And, it seems, Mary felt she could bring in added income for the family by renting out rooms to travelers. Before long, the Donoho houses took the form of an inn. The formidable Mrs. Donoho naturally fulfilled the role of manager, as her husband's trading business required that he travel to other towns to procure needed merchandise and make necessary sales. Apparently, the family was well situated to become leading residents of the city, the first American family to take up residency there.[40]

Meanwhile, eight hundred miles south, another group of pioneer families was about to embark on an adventure near the Rio Grande in the Mexican state of Coahuila, on the east side of the river. In a few years, the area would become part of the Republic of Texas. At this point, the Donohos were not aware of what was transpiring downriver with that group of nearly sixty people at a place newly named Dolores, after the founder's wife. The group in Texas knew nothing about the Donohos or their arrival in Santa Fe. But through circumstances soon to transpire, the Santa Fe family would become intrinsically involved with the Texas pilgrims.

Two people who got caught up in the fever of immigration to America in those years were John and Sarah Ann Horn from London, England. They married on October 14, 1827, when she was only eighteen, and within three years, she had two infant sons, John and Joseph. In mid-1833, they immigrated to the United States, traveling by ship to New York City. It was here that they learned about the unbelievable offer of free land in Texas as promoted by Dr. John Charles Beales, also an emigrant from England.

Husband John decided that the idea of becoming a landowner as promoted by Beales was to his liking. Sarah Ann felt, on the other hand, "notwithstanding all the fortitude I could command, my mind was a constant prey to the most distressing apprehensions." She began to have recurring nightmares about such a venture. Her husband offered to leave her in New

York while he went on alone to establish their new home; then he would return for the rest of the family. She refused to let him go alone, so John signed up to be a colonist in the scheme promoted by the doctor, who in the end was able to interest only fifty-nine people, including men, women and children, to follow him.

Beales had formed a company with others called the Rio Grande Land Company. The plans called for eight hundred willing colonists to each receive 137 acres of free land to help establish a new colony between the Rio Grande and Nueces Rivers in south Texas. He assured prospects that the scheme was in accordance with Mexican colonization policy, and he proceeded to promote it in Europe and the United States.[41]

The group of fifty-nine heading for Texas boarded a ship, the schooner *Amos Wright*, in New York. They sailed around the Florida peninsula and into the Gulf of Mexico, headed for the Texas coast. After disembarking at their promised land, they traveled through several towns: Austin's Colony, La Piedad, San Antonio and Presidio. At each place, the local residents urged them to stay, warning them of the Indian depredations they would experience in the place where they were headed. "We had to keep strict watch every night for fear of Indians, and the Spaniards we regarded as very little better," Sarah Ann said.

Arriving at their destination, they discovered the land was poor desert sand, covered by scrub plants and cactus. The colonists' first order of business was to clear a thicket surrounded by a brush wall as a fortification against the Indians, who were known to be active in the area. Without irrigation to raise crops, the land laid unused for nearly two years. Discouraged by the situation, members of the group began leaving the project. At one point, four families packed up and left, probably headed for the nearest Mexican towns, Monclova, Santa Rosa or San Fernando.

In the winter of 1835, Indians attacked one of the settlements, and four men and a boy were killed. One man was left for dead and scalped. He survived, however, and was taken to the town of San Fernando, where he existed as an object of pity and charity the rest of his life. Eventually, there were only fifteen colonists left on the Texas land, and they were fearful of becoming victims of the Comanches.

The fifteen—eleven men, two women and three children, one an infant child—decided that they, too, must leave for their own safety. Their evacuation route would be overland to the Nueces, then down that river to San Patricio and on to Aransas Bay, the very area where they had disembarked from their ship a couple years earlier.

The Story of the Old Inn at the End of the Trail

Unbeknownst to the straggling party, the countryside was in the midst of war. They did not know that hostilities had broken out between the Mexican government and Texas patriots. Only 140 miles to the north, at San Antonio, the Alamo had fallen to Santa Anna's Mexican army only four days earlier. Remnants of his army were still active along the Nueces. The party camped at the side of the river for several days, all the while within the sound of Mexican soldiers and wagons on the move.

After a couple weeks, they left their camp and followed the river down to a large lake, where they stopped to catch fish. Suddenly, they were attacked by sixty mounted Indians. Nine of the men were instantly killed by the attackers; the two women and their three children were taken captive to the nomadic Indian village, where they became part of an encampment with an estimated population of between three hundred and four hundred people. The other two White men, who they thought were dead at the lakeside, were found alive and brought to the Indian camp.

The two women and the children were forced to watch as the two men were brutally killed. The infant, too, was killed before their eyes, leaving the two ladies, Sarah Horn and Mrs. Harris, horrified, distraught and in shock, especially because one of the men so brutally murdered before them was Mr. Harris. Dr. Beales had somehow left the area and was killed by one of the Mexican platoons some way downriver.

The two women now were captives. At night, their hands and feet were securely tied; during the day, they labored as servants at any warrior's whim or call. They had to sleep on the bare ground and constantly battled mosquitos, but most distressing to Sarah Ann was that her two little boys were taken from her. The next day, they realized they were to become nomads in the tribe's long journey, meandering around West Texas. In time, the multitude traveled to the waters of the Nueces, Guadalupe, Conchos, Colorado, Brazos and Red Rivers. It was a sweltering summer; most of the time, the American women had little or almost no clothing, and starvation seemed always on the horizon, not to mention the constant malicious acts of their captors.

At one point, four-year-old Joseph Horn fell off a mule at a river crossing. His master became angry and with a quick thrust of his knife inflicted a gash just below the boy's eye. Then he threw him back into the river. The boy was able to climb out of the water, thanks to an overhanging branch. Mrs. Horn upbraided the warrior for treating the boy in such a way and for her bravery was whipped by the brute. He then grabbed her hair and with his knife sawed it off. He then tied her hair to his body as a fetish.

At a certain point, the tribe divided into separate parties and began a nearly two-month grueling march. Mother Horn went one way with her group, and her boys went with another part of the tribe in another direction. She would not see her boys, just four and five years old at this time, together again. Her contingent returned to what appeared to her to be their home village. She was assigned to a family that had a senior woman who constantly threw stones or slapped and hit her whenever she felt like it. After too many of these episodes, Horn started throwing the stones back at the old lady. That seemed to even the score between them, and the old lady stopped treating her so badly. Days and months were filled with dressing buffalo robes and deerskins and turning them into garments and moccasins.

Tortured mentally about the whereabouts of her sons, Mrs. Horn was one day told by two little Mexican boys, also captives of the natives, that a little boy had arrived with his captors and that his mother was a prisoner in the camp. She went searching, found him and was able to be with him for a few minutes. But she still did not know the whereabouts of her older son, John. Four months later, at a buffalo hunt, she saw him riding along with other hunters. She was allowed to talk to him for a brief time. It was the last time she ever saw her sons.

The months rolled on, and Horn lost track of time. But an encouraging event took place when "some of Captain Coffee's men came to trade with the Indians and found me." The Texas traders attempted to buy her, but the effort was in vain. Her minders would not sell, even when Captain Coffee himself cajoled and argued for her life. "He expressed the deepest concern at his disappointment and wept over me as he gave me clothing and divided his scanty supply of flour with me and my children, which he took the pains to carry to them himself." Nevertheless, his discovery of these captives would soon become known in important places, through the grapevine of travelers crisscrossing the Southwest.[42]

A little more than four months into captivity, in 1837, a party of Mexican traders came to the camp and began bargaining for the two women's release. The men were colleagues of William Donoho, the American trader whose wife was manager of the inn back on San Francisco Street in Santa Fe. They were successful in freeing Harris, but not Horn. "Now left a lonely exile in the bonds of savage slavery haunted by the image of my murdered husband, and tortured continually by an undying solicitude for my dear little ones, my life was little else than unmitigated misery," she wrote. "The God of Heaven only knows why and how it is that I am still alive," she added.

The Story of the Old Inn at the End of the Trail

Sarah Horn was destined to travel with the tribe three more months as they roamed northward into New Mexico. Then they were only two days travel from San Miguel del Vado at the famous crossing of the Pecos River and only two days travel from Santa Fe. Here there was a large gathering of Indians, apparently to trade with the Pueblo Indians from the Rio Grande Valley and traders from Santa Fe. By this time, the old woman who used to throw stones at her had become quite attached to her and tearfully told Sarah Ann that she thought she would soon be sold to traders at this place.

After three days of trading, the tribe started packing up in preparation to moving back out into the prairies. At that point, a Mexican trader invited Horn's owner to his house and there, amid an array of highly prized gifts, including two fine horses, the nomad was convinced to sell the British woman. "Had I the name of my benefactor I would gratefully record it in letters of gold and preserve it as a precious memento of his truly Christian philanthropy," Horn said. It wasn't long before she would know it was William Donoho.

It was September 19, 1837. She had been a captive of the Comanches for one year, five months and fifteen days.

5
TURMOIL IN SANTA FE

Kindred and home!—E'en [sic] *like yon starving throng,*
Now yearns my bosom for your sympathies,
And like the music of a once-loved song
My heart is teeming with your memories.
Dear home! Your simplest joys seem estacies, [sic]
Even your care now seems a sweet delight.
Thus never till we're plunged in miseries,
Learn we to love and cherish what is bright.
—Matt Field, On the Santa Fe Trail, *288*

Sarah Ann Horn, now a free woman after being taken in by sympathetic New Mexicans for a time, accepted the invitation of a trader family in Taos to stay a while in their home. On her way, she passed through Santa Fe. However, she was not yet aware of her main benefactor, William Donoho, nor did she know that his wife was managing the inn on San Francisco Street. For her part, Mary Donoho apparently did not yet know the particulars of Horn's whereabouts. In time, they would become acquainted, even friends, but not in New Mexico.

Nevertheless, Mary Donoho did know about Sarah Ann's fellow captive, Mrs. Harris. The newly redeemed woman must have learned about the American woman who was running a guesthouse, because she found lodging there and would end up traveling to Missouri with the Donohos, as did another fugitive of the Comanches, Rachel Plummer, who also found sweet relief at the United States House.[43]

The Story of the Old Inn at the End of the Trail

Rachel Parker-Plummer was part of an Illinois religious group called the Predestination Baptist Church that was lured to Texas by the offer of free land in 1833. Their dynamic leader, Daniel Parker, led them to a site on Boxy Creek in eastern Texas. Here they built a stockade fort and began the difficult job of creating farmlands out of virgin forest and grasslands. Feeling secure in their fortress, things went fairly well for the group until May 1836. That's when the Comanches attacked Parker Fort.

The attack took place when the men of the families were busy working the fields. At the time of the raid, Rachel had one son, James Pratt, eighteen months old, and she was pregnant with another. The Indians caught a glimpse of her when she stepped out of the fort enclosure by a side door. The invaders grabbed her infant from her arms, then one warrior beat her unconscious with a hoe. "The first thing I recollect was the Indians dragging me along by the hair of the head," she said. She saw her son once more when he was brought to her for breastfeeding, but when the Indians discovered he was weaned, they took him away again. "This was the last sight I ever had of my little James Platt," she wrote.

She was treated much like Sarah Ann Horn was treated by her captors; she was tied up at night and forced to work dressing buffalo skins and minding the horses during the day. In October, her second child, a son, was born. She named him after her husband, who had been killed in the raid six months earlier. It was then that the most barbaric trial of her imprisonment took place; she was forced to watch the brutal killing of her newborn infant. When its torture ended, she cried, "I was truly glad when I found it was entirely over its sufferings."

Like Horn and Harris, she was forced to serve members of the tribe through its circling meanderings around Texas and into New Mexico, separated from other members of her family, five of whom were also captured in the raid back in May. She estimated that the tribe was well north of Santa Fe when, on June 19, 1837, some Mexican traders showed up at the Indian camp. They commenced to barter with the Indians for her release. Following much haggling and counteroffers, the Indians finally agreed to a deal with the traders. After thirteen months of servitude to the tribe, Rachel was now a free woman.

She made her way to Santa Fe. "I was soon conducted to Col. William Donoho's residence...to whom under the providence of God, I owe my release." Then she met Mrs. Donoho. "I have no language to express my gratitude to Mrs. Donoho. I found in her a mother, a sister to condole with me in my misfortune." It was at the Donoho inn that she soon met Mrs.

Harris, and they became friends, tied together by their common experience. These three women, the only American women in the city at the time, must have found much comfort in their mutual culture and understanding.

Rachel's cousin Cynthia Ann Parker, another of the captives taken at Parker Fort, had no rescuers and ended up a member of the Comanches for twenty-four years. She was taken as a wife by Chief Peta Nocona and became the mother of Quanah Parker, the famous chieftain who fought the encroaching white people but eventually ended hostilities with the Americans in mid-1874, after a final defeat of the Indians at the Second Battle of Adobe Walls in Texas.[44]

Mary Donoho's ministrations to the two rescued women is indicative of her talents as an innkeeper during her four years as manager of the United States House. In those years, nearly one thousand American men, traders and their wagon teams made it to Santa Fe. As they passed the Donohos' inn headed for the main town plaza, they undoubtedly returned to that corner for accommodation if they could afford it and if she had room.[45]

Amid Mary's duties as matron of the inn were added more motherly duties when she bore two more children, Harriet in 1835 and James in 1837. They were the first known American children to be born in New Mexico. Her eldest, Mary Ann, was nearly three years old when her sister Harriet was born. Mary's life was busy, but her inn was her castle, and guests came and went, thankful for the roof over their heads and home-cooked meals.

Social life was good for this first American family, the Donohos, in the New Mexican capital. Several American men who married local Mexican women were residents at that time and became family friends. Life in this unusual city was always interesting, with the comings and goings of wagon trains and the occasional appearance of Native American tribal delegations come to negotiate relationships with the Mexican government. The popular dances, the fandangos, were a regular occurrence, although there is no indication the Donohos participated. There were always unexpected events that made life in the town interesting and in which it seemed everyone was involved; the place was small enough so that anything that happened seemed to catch the interest of everyone.

But if the Donohos had any thoughts of making Santa Fe their permanent home, those thoughts might have faded as they became more familiar with basic infrastructure failings of the place. Schools, for example, were few and operated intermittently or were of dubious quality. Josiah Gregg, the American trader in Santa Fe at the time, said, "the only schools now in existence are of the lowest primary class, supported entirely by individual patronage…at least three-fourths of the present population can neither read nor write." Actions were taken by town officials to retain locally some of the monies going to the church headquarters in Durango down in Mexico proper. Those actions were only on paper, however. It was hoped that the archbishop, who was rumored to soon be making a visit, would sympathize with the situation and permit more funding to stay in the territory to help with educational needs.[46]

Bishop Zubiría had neglected New Mexico for sixty-five years. He arrived from his headquarters in Durango, Mexico, in mid-1833. Of the bishop's arrival, Gregg said the locals "hailed his arrival with as much devotional enthusiasm as if had been the second coming of the Messiah." The city was cleaned and decorated like never before, "streets were swept, the roads and bridges on his route repaired and decorated; and from every window in the city, were hung such a profusion of fancy curtains."

The visit and celebrations lasted several weeks. However, the bishop showed no inclination to improve the educational opportunities or lessen the taxes of the church on the community. Indeed, the cost for marriage ceremonies, baptisms and burials continued to be exorbitant, well beyond what the average citizen could pay. Several months' wages would be needed to acquire such services, relates Gregg. Another historian preserved a bill of $141 presented to a dead man's family by a priest. It would cover the man's burial and, this historian observed, "it is an expensive matter to die and be buried in New Mexico, and it appears to cost quite as much as it does to live."[47]

He watched one day as a poor widow begged a padre for medicine for her sick child. He quoted the mother as saying, "Not that the life of the babe imports me much, for I know the *angelita* will go directly to heaven, but what shall I do to pay the priest for burying it? He will take my house and all from me—and I shall be turned desolate into the street!"

The impoverished condition of the common people, in addition to the daily strain of running a guesthouse, must have tried Susan Donoho constantly. With her husband frequently away on his trading expeditions, she had little day-to-day support in her work. She was the one who had to remain strong in difficult circumstances. But a new challenge was just ahead, one that would make the Missourians decide to retrace their wagon tracks east on the Santa Fe Trail.

In 1836, Mexico adopted a new constitution that brought centralization to its vast provinces, and a new governor, appointed by the government in Mexico City, was sent to be head of state at Santa Fe. He was Colonel Albino

Pérez, a native of Morelia. His appointment was an affront to the people of New Mexico, who had mostly been governed by New Mexicans in the past. The new governor was empowered to impose taxes to fund government operations—new taxes that were highly unpopular.

A few months after the governor's installation, a local government official in Santa Cruz, north of Santa Fe, was charged with embezzlement and was imprisoned. This sparked a series of events that would stand as some of the most barbaric weeks in New Mexico history. The imprisoned man's followers stormed the jail and set him free. They then established a new local government in opposition to the governor. Pérez attempted to quell the uprising and called up a force of supposedly loyal citizens, including many Pueblo Indians, to put down the rebellion. When the troops were ordered to engage with the opposition, most of them deserted to the enemy. In fear, the governor fled back to the capital, only to find the city in an uproar.

He attempted to seek refuge in a ranch south of the city, but he was followed, pursued back to the city and killed on the outskirts. It was August 8, 1837. His body was mutilated, and he was decapitated. His head was taken to the Plaza, where onlookers gasped at the sudden barbarity that had taken over this supposedly most civilized city in the West. Other government officials met the same fate. "About two thousand of the insurgent mob… pitched their camp in the suburbs of the capital," says Gregg. "The inhabitants expected a plundering of the city to follow.…The American traders were particularly uneasy, expecting every instant that their lives and property would fall a sacrifice to the ferocity of the rabble."[48]

The American traders in town feared they would be blamed for encouraging the resurrection. A German American, Charles Blumner, who was in Santa Fe at the time, said the Americans were afraid the revolutionaries would "damage the houses and shops of foreigners. At that time we were about 200 foreign strangers here." They must have gathered in front of the houses that lined San Francisco Street, where their lodgings and shops were located. They were ready for battle, but "saddled horses and mules stood prepared in the courtyards and stables so that we could escape if necessary. But everything proceeded quietly" for them.[49]

The Donohos were aghast at what they had witnessed and, given the turmoil a new native government might cause, decided it was time to leave. They hurriedly started packing up and joined a wagon train heading for the East. Mr. and Mrs. Donoho, their children and the two ladies in their care, Mrs. Harris and Mrs. Plummer, comprised one small party of refugees who joined the worried throng that headed for Missouri. Once there, they

An artist conception of a wagon train on San Francisco Street in Santa Fe. *Postcard in the La Fonda Hotel archives.*

found refuge in the home of a relative in Boonsville. Mr. Donoho then escorted Mrs. Plummer to Texas. Upon his return to Boonsville, he had the opportunity to meet Mrs. Horn for the first time. Both she and Mrs. Harris died within a matter of months from their scars of captivity.[50]

6

SANTA FE REBOUND

In compliment to the American strangers then in Santa Fe, Governor Armijo gave a ball in this grand boarded saloon....All the beauty and fashion attended, and also all the rabble, for, true to their republican principles, none can be refused admission....The governor's lady, Señora Armijo, led off the dance with one of the American guests....The only music is a guitar and violin, and the same instruments are used for sacred music in the churches....Scarcely an evening of the week passes without a fandango.
—Matt Field, On the Santa Fe Trail, *238, 239*

The atrocities and confusion caused by the insurrection that made the Donohos and other American traders' faces turn east on the trail back to Missouri continued for two months, through August and September 1837. To complicate matters, a number of the American traders had extended credit to local businessmen, including those who were murdered, and in the chaos those who remained could not be forced to make good their financial commitments. To add to the upheaval, local instigators of the uprising now claimed and occupied the property previously owned by those leading citizens who had been killed.

As into such calamity opportunists always appear, now a major figure sought the spotlight to take advantage of the confused situation. Enter Don Manuel Armijo. "Probably no man more cruel or unscrupulous ever became prominent in the affairs of the capital," recorded one historian.[51]

Don Manuel Armijo, governor of New Mexico at the time of the Mexican-American War and the American Civil War. *Photograph by Thomas B. Welch, circa 1840. Courtesy of the Palace of the Governors Photo Archives (NMHM/DCA), negative Number 099938.*

General Manuel Armijo.
From a Picture in the Possession of Don Luis Baca, Socorro, New Mexico.

Armijo was "born of low and disreputable parents at or near Albuquerque," said a contemporary historian. "From his earliest childhood his habits were bad. He commenced his career by petty pilfering and as he advanced in years extended his operations until they grew into important larcenies."[52]

As a young man, he made a living by sheep stealing. In 1837, he was appointed collector of customs when the resident collector was accused of peculation (embezzlement). However, that man was exonerated and came back to reclaim his job. Armijo was then unemployed, so he returned to his home in Albuquerque to fume about his treatment by the governor's staff. His brief experience in that office had opened his eyes to what riches were attainable if he could skim off the fees demanded of American traders. He was known by them to be open to bribery and therefore became generally known as a corrupt official.

The tyrant became a central figure in New Mexico for the next eight years. As soon as Armijo heard about the insurrection in August, which he was suspected of encouraging, he returned to the capital expecting that the insurgents would choose him as the new governor. Instead, they chose José Gonzales of Taos. Failing to be acclaimed governor, Armijo began organizing a countercoup, claiming it to be at the behest of the central government in Mexico City. With the help of supporters from the South, he again returned to the capital, took over the Palace of the Governors and proclaimed himself governor.

By late September, with the help of federal troops sent from Chihuahua, he was able to completely rout the rebels. Gonzales, fleeing north to Taos, attempted to approach him to seek peace but was shot dead at Armijo's command. Other conspirators were executed as well. Soon after, Armijo was confirmed governor by the Mexican government, based mostly on his glowing and bloated report of his actions in quelling the disturbance.

Meanwhile, William Donoho headed back to Santa Fe to properly terminate his business activities. Having completed his association with New Mexico in the summer of 1838, he left, never to return. Instead, the Donoho family moved to Texas, where they again engaged in the hotel business and became prominent citizens in Clarksville.[53]

Once again, we are fortunate to have an American writer on the scene to record some of the story of Santa Fe following Armijo's takeover as governor. Arriving in 1839, Matt Field was treated royally. When he and a friend traveled from Taos to the city, they naturally were directed to the American sector. "To the house of Don Luis Rubideau, an American and first Alcalde of Santa Fe, we were duly escorted."

Undoubtedly, he rented space at the United States House, or a nearby house, where the Donohos had recently vacated. He found the houses "very comfortable and by no means inelegant. In winter it is warm, in summer cool." He especially admired the colorful blankets that were used as carpets and tapestries to decorate the interiors. "These blankets are the chief sign of wealth among the people, and their elegance and number forms the pride of every housekeeper."[54]

Field arrived on a Saturday and was quickly introduced to the mayor and had an appointment to meet the governor on Monday. But on Sunday, the alcalde invited him to participate in a social gathering in the establishment of one Señora Toulous. She was Doña Maria Gertrudes Barceló, the leading socialite in town who owned an emporium on Palace Avenue where all kinds of people came to play at cards—one game, the "monte," being the most popular. It seems that other activities took place there as well, but petty gambling seems to have been the main objective. Through her dealing of the monte, she became quite wealthy. "The highest court her favor, and the lowest look at her with wonder. Such is the fine lady of Santa Fe." Field called Toulous "the supreme queen of refinement and fashion."[55]

Entering the Toulous palace, Field and his friend immediately saw Governor Armijo surrounded by his officers. Once polite introductions were complete, a jolly conversation erupted between the governor's Spanish-speaking entourage and the newly arrived English-speaking Field and his friend. Much fun was made of the difficulty the alcalde was having as he struggled to come up with the proper words in both languages to make the conversation meaningful.

The next day, when Field went to meet him, the governor was in good spirits. He announced that he was going to provide a ball for the American traders and visitors. "All the beauty and fashion attended, and also all the rabble, for, true to their republican principles, none can be refused admission," related Field. "It would seem as if the people could not exist without the waltz."[56]

Somewhat normal times returned quite quickly to Santa Fe, but only in the nick of time, as storm clouds were gathering. The governor was about to face a new menace from outside, not inside, the territory. An international incident between Mexico and the new Republic of Texas would soon occupy the minds of residents and military leadership in the capital.

News of the earlier upheaval by the rebels and their ruthless dispatch by Armijo was graphically relayed by travelers and traders to Texas, where the story caused much concern. Texas independence, declared in 1836 after the victorious battle with Santa Anna's army at San Jacinto, included a claim by the new republic to the entire Rio Grande River from source to mouth. The claim was based on an act by the Texas congress that same year. This identified all of New Mexico east of the river as Texas territory. The nearest inhabited New Mexican town to Texas, however, was six hundred miles away at the southern end of the Rocky Mountains, and the claim was not tested during the first five years of the republic, because the new government was busy resolving internal problems of its own.

By 1841, Texas leadership under President Mirabeau Bonaparte Lamar decided to address the situation in Santa Fe. News came to Governor Armijo that a large expedition was forming in Austin that would travel to New Mexico's capital. Volunteers were being recruited through announcements in the *Austin City Gazette*. Its caravan was being called a "mercantile trading enterprise" but was to be escorted by the military. Volunteers were urged to bring their guns and plan on a six-month commitment.[57]

The information about the expedition naturally caused alarm in the New Mexico capital. Was Texas now going to follow up on its claim to most of New Mexican territory? The expedition quickly formed with great enthusiasm in the Texas capital and became known as the "Santa Fe Pioneers." It was believed that the New Mexicans would welcome this intended show of support.

Santa Fe's Fonda

Sketch of a Santa Fe street scene by Theodore Davis. *Postcard in the La Fonda Hotel archives.*

The forming expedition would include six military companies with 270 men, a cannon, 10 leading merchants and the president's commissioners. The crowd included an observer journalist, George Wilkins Kendall of New Orleans. Eighteen wagons would carry trade goods and the needed provisions and supplies.

In a printed broadside to be distributed in New Mexico, the president made it clear that the goal of the assemblage was to "the great River of the North…the natural and convenient boundary of our territory, and we shall take great pleasure in hailing you as fellow-citizens, members of our young Republic." He wrote that he expected the New Mexicans to receive this news in a "spirit of kindness and sincerity."

In mid-June 1841, the expedition set out from Austin. After a jubilant send-off, the mixed group headed north across the vast plains of western Texas and into New Mexico. Their excitement waned as they began to experience the intense heat of the summer sun and the desolation of the terrain. Indian bands were constantly following their progress, ready to attack any small group that should leave the main caravan. Food supplies began to dwindle, and they were forced to scavenge the countryside for something to eat—roots and lizards.

The first members of the expedition to arrive were the president's commissioners; they were immediately put in jail by Governor Armijo. They later escaped, and two were recaptured. The third was soon hunted down and shot on orders from Armijo. Soon, the expedition's entire membership, in their weakened condition and mental fatigue, were captured near San Miguel del Vado.

They were rounded up as prisoners and forced to march to Mexico City under military guard, arriving there in December. About forty of them died on the trail. For over a year, they filled the jails in and around the Mexican capital. They were permitted to return to Texas in 1842. Their anticipated march on Santa Fe never happened, and their attempted takeover of the New Mexico Territory was a dismal failure.

7
NEW MEXICO INVADED

We sang duets, one on one side, and one on the other of the beautiful stream. We sang loud chorusses [sic], *and the lonely woods gave us back a running accompaniment of echos* [sic]. *And when the night-birds screamed, after we had laid our heads upon our saddles to sleep, we laughed at the poor beknighted creatures, and raised our voices in merry imitations of the doleful sounds, till the hungry wolves caught up our cry, and awed us into silence with their dismal howlings.*
—*Matt Field,* On the Santa Fe Trail, *77*

Three years after the return of the Santa Fe Pioneers to Texas in 1845, that republic was annexed by the United States. The event caused apprehension in Santa Fe, as Armijo's gang feared something similar could happen to New Mexico. Indeed, relations between Mexico and the United States became tense as a new president, James K. Polk, was sworn into office in Washington that year. At the same time in Mexico, Santa Anna's dictatorial style began to cause serious political reprisals.

Mexico's attempt to return to constitutional authority came on January 4, 1846, when the country elected a new president, General Don Mariano Paredes. In negotiations with the new president, Polk offered to purchase New Mexico and California. But a new, hawkish president was suddenly elected in Mexico, and negotiations crumbled. News of the change arrived in Santa Fe in February. Governor Armijo attempted to rouse patriotic zeal among the New Mexicans with a proclamation extolling the new president's attributes.[58]

The United States had deployed an army to southern Texas under the command of General Zachary Taylor, sent there in the spring of 1845 to secure the western boundary for the new Lone Star State at the Rio Grande. This was seen as a threat by Mexico, which insisted that the boundary of Texas did not extend that far to the west. The Mexican military was preparing to counter the American threat. On April 26, the Mexicans attacked, killing several officers and their men. Polk now had a reason for America to declare war on its southern neighbor, and the U.S. Congress agreed.

Back in Santa Fe, by early June, Governor Armijo had received reports that an American army was headed toward New Mexico over the Santa Fe Trail. He asked the electoral assembly for money to defend the city, and 1,000 pesos were allocated to oppose the American force. That was the last meeting of the assembly. "One week later Santa Fe was handed over to the American commander…without firing a shot or shedding a drop of blood."[59]

Colonel Stephen Watts Kearny was commander of the U.S. Army's Third Infantry at Fort Leavenworth, Kansas, when the president ordered formation of an army to attack Santa Fe. Kearny was a distinguished officer due to a successful exploratory march that he conducted in 1845 when he and his men traveled west at least 2,200 miles through to the Colorado River and back to Missouri. Because of his familiarity with the western lands of the continent, he was chosen to lead the campaign to Santa Fe. At the end of June 1846, his Army of the West began its trip across the prairies.

Governor Armijo claimed publicly that he had six thousand men ready to prevent any takeover of the New Mexico Territory. In the end, however, mostly due to the softening of the political landscape of New Mexico by agents sent in by the U.S. government, Armijo decided at the last minute not to attempt a confrontation with the invading army. Of most importance in that work of mitigation was American businessman Samuel Magoffin, who previously had been a tradesman resident in Chihuahua. He, with his wife, Susan, accompanied Kearny's army to Santa Fe.

It is Susan Magoffin's diary that gives us the most detailed description of Santa Fe at this time. Her husband, like numerous American tradesmen before him, found a house to rent for their stay, near the corner of the Santa Fe Trail and San Francisco Street. Kearny and his officers found accommodation in the Palace of the Governors, and the soldiers took over the barracks of the ousted Mexican military.

Arriving at the end of August, Susan found her rented house to be very suitable for their needs. It had four rooms, including a kitchen, bedroom, living room/dining room and storage room. It had hard-packed dirt floors

Above: General Stephen Watts Kearney, commander of the U.S. Army unit that liberated New Mexico during the American takeover. *Photograph by Ben Wittick, 1847(?). Courtesy of the Palace of the Governors Photo Archives (NMHM/DCA), negative Number 0007605.*

Opposite: A depiction of the U.S. Army entering New Mexico in 1836. *From a painting by Willard Andrews, courtesy of the New Mexico Capitol Art Foundation.*

The Story of the Old Inn at the End of the Trail

and a plank ceiling. She may not have been aware of it at the time, but a thick covering of earth on the roof was customary. A couple of weeks later, she experienced the fickleness of a mud roof.

She was busy entertaining guests when a rainstorm suddenly developed. She related, "Soon we were leaking all around, the mud roof coming with the water, and had the rain not stoped [*sic*] when it did, we might soon have been left without a canopy."[60] She was also constantly aware that the house was very near a church with annoying bells that were chiming "all the time."[61]

In the same block of houses where the Magoffins were staying was the large square house on the corner owned by the Pino family or their relatives. It was this building that was known as the United States House. It became "the most notable land-mark of the Santa Fe Trail during the 'American' period," asserts one historian. "It was a one-story building built around a patio....It was the rendezvous of trappers, traders, pioneers, merchants, soldiers and politicians."[62]

About this time, a formal entrance to the building was created at the street corner facing the Plaza. Porches, known as *portales*, were added along the San Francisco Street side; along the Old Santa Fe Trail side were private rooms with doors facing the street as well as an inside door leading to a central courtyard. On the south side of the interior courtyard was the hotel dining room and kitchen. Doors on San Francisco Street led into a bar and a large room "in which was to be found every kind of gambling game known in the West," said one observer.

At first, furniture in the inn would have been of the most rudimentary type. One visitor said, "The immense expense attending the purchase of suitable furniture and kitchen-ware, indeed, the frequent impossibility of obtaining these articles at any price," made people in northern Mexico resort to creating their own household tools, usually based on what Native Americans and the Spanish furnished their abodes with—only simple handmade utensils. In most homes, bed mattresses served as couches during the day and then became beds at night, for example. Within a few years, this would change with more cargo brought in from America.[63]

In addition to the new entertainments at the hotel, as in past times, social life for town residents followed a familiar pattern for Santa Fe: frequent dance parties, markets and fiestas took place as they always had. Only now, American soldiers jammed the town square and the festive halls.

An interesting visitor arrived in Santa Fe during this time. He was the aristocratic George Frederick Augustus Ruxton, a member of the British Royal Geographical Society and the Ethnological Society of London, an adventurer who decided to travel solo up through Mexico and New Mexico to the Rocky Mountains. He arrived in Vera Cruz on the Gulf of Mexico on a royal British packet ship and headed into Mexico City, then traveled north on the Camino Real to Santa Fe. His description of the town of three thousand was quite dismissive: "The town is a wretched collection of mudhouses.…The appearance of the town defies description, and I compare it to nothing but a dilapidated brick-kiln or a prairie-dog town."[64]

"Neither was the town improved, at the time of my visit, by the addition to the population of some three thousand Americans, the dirtiest, rowdiest crew I have ever seen collected together," he declared. It was Kearny's volunteer army. "Crowds of drunken volunteers filled the streets, brawling and boasting."

He abhorred the hubbub and unsanitary conditions of the city, so he stayed only a couple of days, preferring to head north for solace in the mountains he was seeking. In his narrative he does not mention entering any of the buildings, and his habit of finding lodging with Mexican or Native American families indicates that he most likely did not seek accommodation downtown. His descriptions of Santa Fe fill only 2 paragraphs in his 331-page book.

Meanwhile, General Kearny, knowing that he had yet to secure more of the West for America, was determined to see that a local government was in place in Santa Fe. In orders dated September 22, 1846, he appointed an administration headed by the well-known trader Charles Bent as governor.

The new governor would split his time with the government at Santa Fe and his family at home in Taos. With this capable man in charge, the general felt he could leave for the West, where California waited to be conquered.

On September 25, the soldiers said goodbye to the city, for they were on their way to California. Their main scout for the trip was Kit Carson, the most knowledgeable man in all of the West for that duty. His excellent knowledge of the desert and his daring in battle would help save the day at the Battle of San Pasqual northeast of San Diego. When Kearny's troops were surrounded by Californians, Kit, along with a Native American believed to be from a California tribe, and Lieutenant Edward Beale snuck through enemy lines barefoot and hiked thirty miles to San Diego Bay to get reinforcements from a U.S. Navy ship that was anchored there, thus becoming the heroes of the Battle of San Pasqual.[65]

The Magoffins departed Santa Fe shortly after the army left town. They were headed for Chihuahua on their extended trading expedition. James Magoffin left with the knowledge that he had played a very important part in securing the American Southwest for the conquerors. In a few months, he would hear news of the end of the Mexican-American War.

On February 2, 1848, the Treaty of Guadalupe Hidalgo ended hostilities between Mexico and the United States. After two years of battles, most of them taking place in Mexico itself, the Southwest was now officially part of the United States. In the process, the United States gained the two huge territories of New Mexico and California. The war also settled the question of the Texas border, defined as the Rio Grande River from the Gulf of Mexico up to New Mexico's southern border. Santa Fe was now a secure American territorial capital city. Or so the residents thought.

With the takeover of New Mexico by the Americans, the English language began its inexorable climb in importance at the same time that connections with the eastern states increased, especially with the permanent installment of the military at a new fort, Fort Marcy, on the northern perimeter of the city. On March 3, 1847, a congressional act authorized the making of a contract for Pony Express mail service between Independence and Santa Fe.[66]

And the printed page arrived, thanks to the delivery of a new printing press. Two men, one said to be a military volunteer who decided to stay and begin a new life in the capital, Hovey and Davis launched the first English-language newspaper, the *Santa Fe Republican*. The first issue appeared on September 10, 1847. It was the first attempt at publishing a newspaper that had permanence. And it's thanks to the *Republican* that we gain more information about the Inn at the End of the Trail.[67]

In June 1848, the newspaper printed an advertisement about the United States Hotel, submitted by its new lessees: Humphrey and Coulter. These two Americans sensed the potential for a profitable investment in the old fonda in this city that would grow substantially now that it was in American hands. The newspaper announced that the two new managers leased the hotel and had "thoroughly repaired and renovated the same," estimated by one observer to cost the duo $10,000. Humphrey and Coulter claimed that the hotel was "well supplied with beds and large ventilated rooms." The ad also mentioned that the hotel had the only corral for animals in the city. The corral was located at the back of the building bordering Rio Chiquito, later Water Street.[68]

To operate the hotel, two gentlemen were hired: Frank Green and Thomas Bowler. They were known as "very popular caterers." According to an observer at the time, "Owing to the lack of well-trained help…Green… made a trip to Chihuahua for the purpose of securing help for their hostelry." In the process, he returned to Santa Fe with "two expert bartenders, a half dozen table waiters…and a number of well-trained musicians." This group soon set the standard for hospitality and entertainment in the city.[69]

Business was good at the United States Hotel. Rooms were full, the dinner tables were well attended and the games of chance kept people occupied. But a new revolt was brewing; things never stayed calm in Santa Fe for very long. Just as the Native Americans resented the takeover of New Mexico by the Spanish over two hundred years before, now the established Spanish aristocrats resented the takeover by the Americans.

8
SANTA FE BOOMS

The sun was just setting when we rode into the large square of Santa Fe and shook hands with the American storekeepers. Here we were after our two months pilgrimage, arrived at last in the strange place to which our wild love of novelty had led us, and as we gazed round upon a race of beings that seemed not like the inhabitants of earth and yet were on it…a buoyant excitement tingled through our veins.…To meet here brothers with whom we could exchange greeting in our native tongue was another charm to heighten our satisfaction, for what delight is dearer to the heart or half so welcome as the hand of a brother in a foreign land?
—Matt Field, On the Santa Fe Trail, *203*

The United States Hotel, arguably the first hotel in Santa Fe, became the focal point of society during its two years of existence under that name. The influx of U.S. Army soldiers was the impetus that initially brought much popularity to the place, in the Santa Fe boom period of the 1850s. "Journals of officers with the occupying army record many *bailes*, or dances, and dinners and social gatherings," says one historian.

A major event at the beginning of the American occupation was a ball given in honor of General Sterling W. Price, who arrived in October 1846, as new commander of the Santa Fe garrison. The *Republican* reported about the ball, "all enjoyed it as much from the overflowing of their joy at the arrival of Gen. Price as from the good accommodations and very agreeable company present."[70]

We know of the men in charge at the hotel, but also mentioned was a "hostess." It may have been Mrs. G. Habile. Credit should go to the male managers for evidently sensing the need for a woman's touch about the place; they hired this congenial lady from New Orleans to be proprietress of the establishment. The newspaper reported that she "will be pleased to receive a few more gentlemen as boarders and flatters herself that her efforts to please will, as heretofore, succeed." She was the first woman to appear on the hotel scene since Susan Donoho left for Missouri.[71]

If it was not Habile, the hostess may have been Dona Tules, famous madam of the Monte casino, for one man in town at the time later recollected the hotel musicians were of "Pancho's Band; the latter being of order of Dona Tules Barcelona who had been a well-known habituee [sic] of the...hotels for many years."[72]

As for General Price, he soon was informed of rising local discontent with the new American government by a considerable number of the longtime Spanish leaders in the capital. Rumors of a planned revolt were confirmed, confronted and quashed in Santa Fe. But then the discontent migrated north to Taos, where a conspiracy against the government continued to foment. Certain discontents were calling for the ouster or death of the American officials who had been installed by General Kearny.

The turmoil in the North was a concern to Governor Bent, but he was not worried that things would get out of hand, for he knew the people well—he was one of them, he reasoned. But he was worried about his family up in Taos and decided that he should bring them to safety in Santa Fe. He and a cadre of associates, including a sheriff, left for Taos in the middle of January 1847.

He was comforted to find his family safe at home and happy to see him. They all went to bed that night, content that he was now there to protect them. Early the next morning, however, the governor received an urgent warning that a mob was headed for his house. He quickly dressed and headed to a side window. On jumping to the outside, he was pierced by two arrows. He stumbled back into the house, where intruders had broken through the door. He was shot two times. Governor Bent died, but his family was spared.[73]

The rampage and killings continued at towns in the area around Taos. Colonel Price mustered the army, about 400 soldiers strong, to march north to Taos. He discovered several of the insurgents were seeking asylum at the Taos Pueblo Church. The army proceeded to bombard the church with canon, killing 150 of the people inside. Several skirmishes at other locations finally subdued the insurrection, and by 1848, Colonel Price could report that all was calm again in New Mexico.

Despite New Mexico's internal difficulties, as it often happens, good and bad can appear together. The good that came, especially for the United States Hotel, was news that gold had been discovered in California, an event that would effect changes in faraway Santa Fe. The news about gold spread by early 1849, and eastern people called "49ers" began to flood the Santa Fe Trail with a new breed of the human wave: would-be miners. The well-worn established Santa Fe route began to attract thousands of men anxious to make their fortune in the gold fields. They liked the idea that a civilized stop was expected in Santa Fe before crossing the wide expanse of the New Mexico desert that stretched to the Grand Canyon and on to the Colorado River to the California border.

What's more, New Mexico was now a U.S. territory, and Americans could not contemplate that there would be any objections to their free passage all the way to the West Coast. But the route was through Native American tribal lands. Stories of atrocities and killings abounded in Santa Fe about battles between the wagon trains and the tribes who fought the incursion of the Americans into their territories and hunting grounds. Their battle to maintain control of their lands and keep the foreigners out would continue for centuries.

The Santa Fe Trail "was more dangerous than it had been in its crystal dawn, when Becknell first rode over it," said one historian. "But the Indians could not dam back the white flood." He shared the report by a military officer at the time who counted three thousand wagons, twelve thousand people and fifty thousand head of stock pass by his post in one year on the trail.[74]

But the surge in visitors to Santa Fe, most of them only stopping to provision their wagons for the remainder of their trip, meant more demand for proper overnight rooms, baths and food. The Inn at the End of the Trail was in great demand, and competition was coming. In June 1848, the *Republican* carried notice of a new boardinghouse, the Missouri House, opening on San Francisco Street. Later in the year, another guesthouse, the Independence House, was advertised.

At the United States Hotel itself, changes were taking place. It received a new name, the Exchange Hotel. In 1849, new managers by the names of Raymond and Wood spruced up the building and brought much-needed refinements from the East. The owners "respectfully announce to the friends and the traveling community that they have gone to great expense and labor to guarantee them that comfort, ease and pleasure which cannot possibly be found at any other hotel this side of the City of St. Louis." To add to the enticements, they "also have three splendid Billiard Tables… and…Ten-Pin Alley."[75]

For some reason, it seems that Raymond and Wood's reign at the hotel was short-lived, because records show that in 1850, Francisco Ortiz and Delgado signed a lease contract with two Americans by the names of Rumley and Ardinger. The transitions during this time may have involved the different houses belonging to several families who owned them at this hospitality corner of Santa Fe; official records are somewhat confusing during this time. A year later, there was a fire of some consequence at this location, and another lease was transferred to Francisco Baca and a Mr. S.C. Florence. Nevertheless, the boarding of increasing numbers of visitors was a huge challenge in the city.[76]

Not only were wagon trains on the trail increasing exponentially, communication with the East was also greatly improved with the inauguration of monthly stagecoach service between Independence and Santa Fe. The stages were "beautifully painted and made water-tight," reported the Independence newspaper *Missouri Commonwealth*. They were also built to give the passengers as much comfort as possible. Mark Twain, describing his experience, said, "Our coach was a greate [sic] swinging and swaying stage of the most sumptuous description—an imposing cradle on wheels." He was referring to the large oxhide leather straps that stretched beneath the passenger cabin.[77]

Drivers of the stages and of the covered wagons had the penchant for making as much of a show as possible as they entered their destination city. One of the most famous, Wild Bill Hickok, was known as one of the most successful stage drivers of the time, mainly because of his daring and rifle marksmanship. Stories of his ability to outsmart several stagecoach robbers became legend. Whenever his stage entered Santa Fe, "it was his habit to treat the passengers to 'a shaking up,' as he styled it, in 'order to jolt the cricks out of their backs.'"

The Santa Fe Trail, as it neared its end at Santa Fe, was Hickok's favorite place to act the daredevil. "There was a slight decline, and so Wild Bill invariably turned the horses loose and gave them the lash," said biographer Frank Wilstach. "So it was that the big coach bounded along 'lurching the passengers from side to side, dishing up dyspeptics, phlegmatics [sic], and rollicking dispositions indiscriminately, and bowling into the town finally the centre [sic] of a dust bank and the object of excited interest to everyone in the ancient Mexican city.'"[78]

An Overland Stage on display at Boggsville Historic Site near the confluence of the Arkansas and Purgatoire Rivers in Colorado. *Author's collection*.

Hickok was a driver with the Overland Stage Company for a short time, then he joined the wagon trains from Independence as a hired driver. In his travels he became friends with Buffalo Bill Cody, eventually signing up as part of Cody's Wild West Shows, where his expert use of a gun was put on display, much like Annie Oakley, who became known as the fastest female gun in the West.

It was the practice of stage drivers, upon arrival at Santa Fe, to halt in front of the Exchange Hotel, "and the passengers, with bag and baggage, were turned over to the custody of 'mine host,' who stood at his threshold, in the best possible humor, to receive us," wrote W.W.H. Davis about his arrival. While he said he could not compare the place to the Astor Hotel back East, "withal, it seemed an admiral change to us, who for nearly a month, had been exposed to the discomforts of the Plains." He complimented the hotel on an excellent spread at the dinner table.[79]

Santa Fe's Fonda

The arrival of the Overland Stage in front of the Exchange Hotel always provided excitement in the city. *Postcard in the La Fonda Hotel archives, printed by Southwest Arts & Crafts.*

Another new arrival in town in 1851 was James A. Bennet, a young recruit in the U.S. Army from Texas. On his first evening, he was enjoying a relaxing break in the Exchange when "a person came in, took a glass of brandy, turned from the bar and commenced firing his pistol at random, and could not be stopped until he had fired four shots." Four people were wounded, including a lawyer shot in the abdomen and another man shot in the arm.

When asked why he started shooting, Bennet reported, "A friend of his from Texas was killed at Santa Fe, and all inhabitants of the place were cutthroats, robbers and murderers." The man was put in jail but later was taken from the jail and hanged in the back stable yard of the Exchange.[80]

Among the many visitors to arrive in Santa Fe in 1851 was a most distinguished gentleman. The people of Santa Fe were in a holiday mood on August 9. Everyone was dressed in their best Sunday clothes, banners and beautiful rugs and blankets were hung from every window and everyone was heading to the edge of town on the Camino Real. They were there to welcome one of the most important new members of the Santa Fe scene. A new bishop was arriving from the East.

Archbishop Jean-Baptiste Lamy, 1875–80. *Courtesy of the Palace of the Governors Photo Archives (NMHM/DCA), negative Number 065116.*

Catholic priest Jean-Baptiste Lamy, a Frenchman, was appointed bishop of New Mexico by Pope Pius IX on July 19, 1850. He began planning his trip from his home base at Covington, Ohio—he would take the long route by boat on the Ohio and Mississippi Rivers down to New Orleans, then hop a ship to the Texas coast. There was a major mishap when the ship arrived at Matagorda Bay: it sank within sight of land when trying to cross a sandbar.

Lamy made it to shore with one hundred other passengers in lifeboats. Fortunately, he spotted his trunk full of books amid the debris floating at the shore and was able to recruit another man's help to retrieve it. From the coast, he traveled overland 140 miles to San Antonio, where he joined a military caravan headed for Santa Fe. His trip lasted many months. Finally, on this warm August day, he was about to enter the city that he had only heard of and dreamed about.[81]

As they came within sight of the city with the backdrop of the Rocky Mountains, Lamy guessed there might be a welcoming committee to meet him. But much to his astonishment, thousands of people lined the roadway, starting five miles out from town. He first thought they were there to welcome the military unit but soon realized they were there to accompany him to his church at the end of San Francisco Street.

The huge throng led him the length of that street, parading past the Plaza and the Exchange Hotel to the Church of St. Francis. From the army at Fort Marcy, cannon sounded a bombastic welcome salute. Celebrations continued the rest of the day and into the night. New Mexico now had its own bishop! He would become famous for his spiritual and civic leadership and community works and in time would build a new cathedral, establish boys' and girls' schools and turn his residence into Santa Fe's first hospital.[82]

9
THE TRAIL TO CALIFORNIA

The Camp is still. Now stalks the guard
Around the mules on duty hard.
And as he slowly moves about
He sees the fires go glimmering out;
While o'er the grass the chill night dew
Falls till his boots are well soaked through.
Small stakes are driven in the ground
For the tired mules to graze around
Lest they should wander out of sight
And Indians steal them in the night.
At dawn the sleepy travelers rise
Before the stars have left the skies,
Before the sun sends forth a ray
The Camp is struck, the teams away.
—Matt Field, On the Santa Fe Trail, *41*

The two men could hardly have been more different. Leonard Rose was twenty-two years old, of German background and of slight build. A businessman, he was always a man in charge. Alpha Brown, thirty-three, was "a poor man but a noble man nevertheless, and was a highly respected man." He decided to join the gold rush of 1849, "and despondent over the passing of his wife, traveled to California to seek his fortune. In two years, he was back…with no gold but 'rich in experience.'"[83]

The two men became friends in their adopted Keosauqua, Iowa, where Rose was a successful retailer. "He became a mercantilist, trading goods up and down the Mississippi River, and opened his own general store." Brown became a handyman. He remarried at this time. His new wife, the widowed Mary Fox, had four daughters, the oldest twelve-year-old Sarah, whom everyone called "Sally." Soon, a new son was born to the Browns.[84]

The two men decided to become business partners and started planning. They both had a desire to move to California. In the winter of 1856–57, they formed a partnership. According to their agreement, "Rose would provide the funds necessary to outfit an emigrant train, and Brown, because of his experience crossing the country, would manage the expedition."[85]

They advertised for a crew of men to accompany the caravan, and seventeen, of various ages but most under thirty, "jumped at the chance." They would drive the wagon teams and serve as herders and fulfill their dreams of finding gold in California if all went well. Rose was dreaming of starting a ranch in the Golden State—a dream he would one day fulfill. Brown just wanted to farm in a warmer climate—unfortunately, he would not realize his dream.

In planning their trip, they decided to avoid going through Utah because of what was called the "Mormon Troubles." Brigham Young had led his followers out to that region and threatened to start a new state with him as governor, much to the objection of the U.S. government. It was thought that intruders could be in danger if they entered into potential battle areas of Utah. The safest route seemed to be to Santa Fe and Albuquerque and then through western New Mexico to the California border.[86]

In the spring of 1858, the Rose-Brown wagon train headed for Kansas and on to New Mexico with 3 horses, 14 trotting mares, 6 mules and 140 head of cattle and oxen. They had four heavy prairie schooner wagons and a carriage that Rose called an "ambulance."[87]

In late May, the emigrant train rumbled into Kansas City. There they admitted a family of five who also wanted to travel west. By the time the caravan reached Santa Fe, six other families had joined. It was now what could be considered a large wagon train, with twenty wagons, forty men and nearly sixty women and children. The animals in the entourage included twelve mules, five hundred head of cattle and several milk cows, in addition to Mr. Rose's horses.

After traveling three months, the train neared Santa Fe and split into two groups. One group, mostly men, bypassed the city with the animals and headed south for Albuquerque. The other group, including most of the women and children, continued into the old city. "One can readily believe that the women fairly reveled in a shopping expedition, the first in three months," wrote L.J. Rose Jr. in the biography of his father. The elder Rose apparently was impressed with Santa Fe, because he soon decided to return. It's possible he even treated his family to an overnight stay at the Exchange Hotel on this first visit.[88]

At Albuquerque, the regrouped wagon train leaders tried to find out as much about the trail west as possible. They learned that a trail had indeed been opened recently by Lieutenant Edward Beale. Camels imported from the Middle East were used by Beale to establish the route. Secretary of War Jefferson Davis approved the purchase and import of these animals: he was assured they would do very well in conquering the desert trails of America's West.

However, Rose and Brown were warned that even though it was the best trail heading west, only one man had traveled it before: Edward Beale. He was reportedly about to return to Albuquerque with more camels to improve marking the trail to California. The local military commander also insisted that the Rose-Brown train would not be permitted to leave without a guide. They hired a man by the name of José Manuel Saavedra, who had served Beale when he first marked the route but then had been punished by the trail maker for his incompetence.[89]

The military leader also warned the group to keep their wagons close together as they traveled, and he said no one should wander far from the train. This would help discourage any Indian observers from attacking. Local citizens assured the travelers that they would encounter no dangers once they crossed the Colorado into California. However, they warned, the Mojave tribal lands were located in the vicinity of the Colorado and they therefore should be alert to danger in that area.

Unbeknownst to Rose and Brown, the threat of a "Mormon War" on the more northern route was being resolved at the same time that they were in Albuquerque learning about the Beale trail. After they set out from Albuquerque, news of the successful negotiations between the Mormons and the U.S. government appeared in the New Mexican newspapers. In exchange for religious freedom and permission for Brigham Young to be its religious leader, the Utah Territory would become part of the United States with a new governor appointed by the U.S. president.[90]

While the armistice between Utah and the United States averted hostilities between the two parties, the tribes along the Colorado River had long been warned by Mormon scouts that more white people would be coming into their territory. It was an attempt to gain the Native Americans' assistance in combating U.S. forces in the event of an incursion into Utah by the U.S. military.

The news that more Americans would be coming alarmed the Indian tribes, who feared they would lose their tribal homelands. The Mojave tribe especially feared that its lands would be invaded and colonized by the Americans. Beale's trail was seen by them as a means of access to more incursions into their territory. They realized they would have to fight to protect their land.

It was in this context that the first wagon train to try Beale's route was the Rose-Brown group, which set out from Albuquerque in the summer of 1858. Their journey would take them through the arid half of New Mexico, about five hundred miles across. On their route, they would pass through only two settlements, a herder's station and the village of Zuni. "They started rolling toward the Colorado River, not fully understanding what might be waiting."[91]

Their troubles began quite early. "The mountain travel made the cattle foot-sore, and beyond the mountains they often had to make forced marches in the heat," wrote seventy-year-old J.W. Cheney, who wrote about the adventure in 1915. They were constantly on the search for water and enough grass to feed 260 cattle and oxen.[92]

A Mojave family at their wikiup on the Colorado River. *Photograph by Ben Wittick, 1883(?). Courtesy of the Palace of the Governors Photo Archives (NMHM/DCA), negative Number 015966.*

About eighteen miles from the Colorado River, three teams of oxen pulling wagons collapsed from weakness. A decision was made that the Rose and Brown families would travel ahead to the river with their cattle and herders, leaving the others until their oxen recovered or until the forward group sent messengers back that the way was clear for them to travel onward.

Suddenly, just a couple of miles from the river, the advance party was surrounded by Indians. "They were smiling and laughing. The emigrants relaxed." Twenty-five warriors accompanied them to the river, but several fires blazing at the river's edge roused the suspicions of the American party. They soon discovered that the warriors were planning a barbecue when they separated several cows from the herd, killed them and started roasting the meat.[93]

Rose and Brown, not knowing how many warriors they would have to battle, decided that retaliation against the Native Americans for their thievery would not be wise. The next day, a Mojave chief and his entourage appeared at their camp and inquired as to how long they intended to stay in the area. Rose assured him they merely wanted to cross the river and travel into California. Permission was granted.

For about two days, the wagon train occupants went about their daily chores of cleaning up after meals, washing clothes in the river and preparing for the next meal. Some children were playing around the wagons, others were napping. "For a while everything seemed peaceful that hot August afternoon at Beale's Crossing."

Suddenly, Alpha Brown's daughter Sally saw warriors darting between the trees, and she noticed they were carrying bows and arrows. She yelled, "The Indians are coming! They are going to kill us all!" Once discovered, the Indians attacked, screaming and yelling. Arrows began falling from the sky by the hundreds.

The migrants thwarted the first attack with quick gunfire; seven warriors soon lay dead on the ground. Three children in the camp lay dead. At the time of the attack, Alpha Brown was by the river helping several men construct a raft for the water crossing. At the sound of gunshots from the camp, he mounted his horse and headed back to camp. As he dashed through the warrior group he was hit by several arrows, one close to his heart. He made it to the campsite but then fell from his horse and died.

The warriors then retreated, leaving the defenders to contemplate their situation. The whites counted six of their number dead, three seriously wounded and eight with superficial wounds. They still had enough gunpowder for one more battle, but such an event, they realized, would be a disaster.

They concluded that they had only one hope: return to Albuquerque. At 5:00 p.m., they began retracing their steps across the desert. "No one looked back at the deserted camp, where five large wagons, loaded with all their worldly possessions, sat unattended, waiting for new owners."[94]

In one-hundred-degree heat, the migrants trudged across the desert, their shoes and boots giving out. They were counting their days until death when they excitedly met a wagon train from Iowa heading west, commanded by a friend of Rose, Mr. Hamilton. The newcomers shared their water and food with the weary group and, on hearing the details of their experience, decided to return to Albuquerque with them.

When they arrived at Zuni, the residents quickly prepared emergency food and shelter. On November 1, 1858, sixty-one days after the massacre, the United States Army from Albuquerque came to the rescue at Zuni with wagons loaded with food, shoes and clothing. By the middle of November, the survivors of the ordeal arrived at Albuquerque, where they were sheltered and fed by locals.

The Rose and Brown families lost all their material goods in the venture, and Mary Brown lost her husband and youngest child. Rose still had his carriage and horses, Old Bob and Picayune, to pull it. They would take him on a successful trip to California in a couple of years.

"L.J. Rose worked in Albuquerque a short time as a waiter, then moved his family to Santa Fe." With funds borrowed from a brother-in-law in the East, in 1858, he purchased the hotel and bar called the Exchange Hotel. They soon refreshed the old building and instigated German cleanliness and order. It seems the old inn had a poor reputation at this time. "But as a good businessman, Rose turned the place into a true money-maker and sold it for a large profit." The Rose family claimed Santa Fe as home for nearly two years. In 1861, when rumors of war coming to Santa Fe were circulating, "the Rose family…resumed their journey to California. They made it safely this time."[95]

10
ANOTHER INVASION

We sat in a trader's store, and an old trapper, with a long iron-grey beard, was telling us his exploits in the mountains. The monotonous and unmusical tune, played upon the drum and fife, by the two soldiers who parade the great square, announcing eight o'clock, had ceased nearly an hour, and all outside was still even as midnight. Suddenly loud screams and yells reached us from some street…and we had scarcely time to spring to our feet before several pistol shots were heard in rapid succession. We darted into the street and met a dozen soldiers.
—*Matt Field,* On the Santa Fe Trail, *240*

Some people said Henry would have made a better politician than a soldier. He was a very complex person. Happy at times, sour at others. Anyone who became his friend soon found they were in a love/hate relationship. His unpredictable personality was a challenge to friends and enemies. Yet, here he was in the year 1861, a brigadier general in the Confederate army.[96]

Henry Hopkins Sibley was born on May 25, 1816, in Natchitoches, Louisiana, to John and Margaret Sibley. They were among the upper classes in the area and had a team of servants to help run their big house in the city's environs. The town was located on the banks of the Red River, a major artery for transportation by riverboat to points west. It was also a major trans-shipping point on the way to San Antonio. The family also owned property west of town among the piney woods of western Louisiana that served as a place of retreat during the hot, humid summers of Natchitoches.

Young Henry was duly impressed by the soldiers marching through town pursuing new assignments in the country's western frontier. Fort Seldon, not far away, was commanded by Colonel Zachary Taylor, and a new military base was soon established at Cantonment (Fort) Jesup. He also had ample opportunity to observe and visit Native American villages and encampments of nearby tribes, first in Louisiana and later in Texas. He developed a keen interest in and appreciation for their lifestyle.

By 1826, however, his world was turned upside down: with the death of his father, his mother lost all of the family's land and possessions in near bankruptcy.[97] In 1828, she moved the family to Missouri to be closer to her family. Two years later, Henry was sent to school in Ohio at Miami Grammar School. The school had seventeen rigid rules and served as Henry's first experience in regimental training. After two years, young Henry applied for admittance to the U.S. Military Academy at West Point, New York, and was accepted. His military life began. The academic curriculum required a summer encampment, where they learned military tradition and tactics. They lived in tents and constantly drilled in marching.

After five years, in 1833, Henry graduated from the academy, thirty-first in a class of forty-five. He was commissioned as a second lieutenant in the U.S. Army.[98] During his early career, he served in the swamps of Florida, the rain forests of Mexico and the wide plains of Kansas.

It is thought that it was during his duty in Mexico that the major began his notorious drinking habit. During these assignments, he was constantly criticized by superiors for failing to submit complete and readable reports that he sent to headquarters.

After the Mexican-American War, he was sent to major cities on the East Coast to enlist new army recruits, including Baltimore, Boston and Utica and Rochester, New York. He then requested reassignment to Texas. His wife and three children accompanied him. On the way to San Antonio, his young son turned gravely ill and died.

In Texas, Henry became commander of several military camps along the Brazos River. "It was while Henry was at Fort Belknap that a rather incidental event was to turn his interests toward military innovation and later place his name on the lips of many a soldier around a frontier encampment or Civil War bivouac."[99]

He invented a tent, known as the "Sibley Tent," that could be used in the field by the dragoons; it became part of military kit and history. It was a cone-shaped affair held up with a single center pole that was supported by a metal tripod that could straddle a fire or stove in the middle of the tent. The canvas tent could accommodate up to twenty men overnight, he claimed. He successfully filed for a patent, No. 14714, on April 22, 1856.[100]

In addition, he patented a small, lightweight heater stove that could nicely provide warmth to all corners of the tent in cold weather. All the components were collapsible so as to save space in transport. It weighed thirty pounds and was thirty-six inches high. As a U.S. military officer holding a patent, Henry was to receive five dollars for every tent that was sold. The U.S. Army ordered nearly 94,000 Sibley tents and stoves during the Civil War; his take would have easily gained him a half million dollars.[101]

Another Sibley invention never caught much attention. It was an artillery shell, the "Sibley Projectile." The innovation was actually "in the sabot, the separate end of the shell that helps it fit in the gun's barrel, and the cotton wadding around the bottom half of the shell." The great idea "was that the cotton would be soaked in lubricant—as the gun was fired, sending the shell up the barrel, the cotton wadding would grip the grooves on the inside of the barrel, both improving the aim and trajectory of the shot and cleaning the barrel at the same time." The U.S. Army had no interest in this, patent No. 225,650.[102]

In 1857, Henry was forty-one years old when he was assigned to lead an expedition against the defiant Mormons in Utah. When that duty was completed, he was ordered south with his company of dragoons into New Mexico, where the U.S. government was hoping to end a continuing fight with the Navajos. In August 1860, he arrived at Santa Fe's Fort Marcy with his First Dragoons. From there, he went to Albuquerque. From there, a war with the Navajos was to be launched.

General Henry Hopkins Sibley, commander of the Confederate army that invaded New Mexico during the Civil War. *United States Library of Congress, Prints & Photographs Division.*

A sketch of the Sibley Tent, invented by General Sibley and widely used by the U.S. Army. *From a travel booklet, the* Prairie Traveler, *published in 1859.*

During the rest of his time in New Mexico, Henry traversed most of the northern landscapes of the territory, including several months in Taos. Idleness and drunkenness plagued the army recruits at this place. At that town, he at one point sought the assistance of Kit Carson and his Ute scouts to join his troops in a sortie against the Plains Indians. In March 1861, a peace treaty was signed with the Navajos. Shortly thereafter, the southern states of the United States began seceding from the union. Texas sided with the Confederacy; New Mexico chose to be a Union territory.

Henry wrote to his wife, who was still in New York, about his desire to go south to help the rebel cause. She pleaded with him to remain loyal. "The possibility of a high-ranking commission in the Confederate Army and the defense of Southern culture, states' rights, and honor, were overwhelming for the brevet major." On April 28, 1861, he resigned from the U.S. Army.[103]

He arranged a leave of absence and traveled to Santa Fe, where he enjoyed the traditional hospitality of the old city for a short time. Then, at El Paso, he felt relieved that his twenty-three-year career in the U.S. Army had come to an end. While in El Paso, Sibley had a chance to philosophize with other Southern sympathizers, including James Magoffin, the Santa Fe trader who now owned a large trading post near El Paso. Sibley then returned to his old stomping grounds in Louisiana.

From New Orleans, he traveled to Richmond to meet with the newly proclaimed president of the Confederacy, Jefferson Davis, with whom he had much in common. "Both had graduated from West Point and fought in the Mexican war together. The two became even better acquainted while Davis was serving as Secretary of War…during which time Sibley had been pushing for the adoption of his tent."[104]

In his interview with the president, Henry demonstrated extensive knowledge of New Mexico and its resources as well as the disposition of the Federal army there. He assured Davis that he could raise a creditable army and that a campaign, his campaign, into New Mexico would be self-sustaining. Southern loyalists would provide food, and his army could forage the countryside to augment what the locals could not provide. After conquering New Mexico, his plan called for heading to the gold and silver mines of Colorado and then launch out for California. He confidently predicted that all of the American Southwest would become Confederate territory.

Davis was delighted with the plan as outlined by Sibley. He rewarded his friend with a commission as brigadier general. He was confident that Sibley would drive the Federal troops from New Mexico and greatly enlarge Confederate holdings all the way to the Pacific coast. He then wished Sibley Godspeed.

"An army under my command enters New Mexico, to take possession of it in the name and for the benefit of the Confederate States. By geographical position, by similarity of institutions by commercial interests, and by future destinies New Mexico pertains to the Confederacy," read the proclamation by Sibley. Early in February 1862, he began his march up the Rio Grande from El Paso.[105]

After an encounter with Federal forces at Fort Craig, where Lieutenant Colonel R.S. Canby was commanding officer, and a regiment of New Mexico volunteers under Colonel Kit Carson were based, he challenged the fort's inhabitants to a battle. In the Battle of Valverde that ensued, Federal losses were sixty-eight killed, while Texan losses were thirty-six dead. Sibley was anxious to leave the scene for greater prizes and ordered his troops north to Albuquerque and Santa Fe.[106]

"One factor working against Sibley was the severe New Mexico winter which continued to impede the progress of the Army of New Mexico," says Sibley biographer Jerry Thompson. "As the campaign began to falter, alcohol became a problem. From all indications General Sibley was not the only one in the Army of New Mexico to overindulge in the 'ardent spirits.'"[107]

In the Battle of Glorieta Pass, the Confederates basically won the day but lost the battle when the Federals, under Major John M. Chivington, were able to turn the tide when they attempted to circle the Confederates to attack from behind and, instead, came upon the rebel wagon train in Apache Canyon just east of Santa Fe. They were able to totally destroy the train, eighty wagons of food, supplies and ammunition, ending Confederate hopes of further action. The ragged and weary Confederate army began a retreat into the city. Some of the rebels "rode, some walked and some hobbled in," past the Exchange Hotel, reported the *Santa Fe Gazette*.[108]

Meanwhile, General Sibley apparently remained in Albuquerque sixty miles to the south through the early days of the campaign. A courier brought news of the battle. "Evidently misinformed and possibly drunk, the general appeared excited by the news and decided to celebrate the occasion." He then headed to Santa Fe himself to evaluate the situation, finding that all government officials had been evacuated north to Las Vegas. In the capital, Sibley was delighted to see old friends from his service time in the city. "While in the capital, General Sibley was drunk a large part of the time," wrote Thompson.[109]

According to historian Ralph Emerson Twitchell, General Sibley, Colonel A.M. Jackson and staff were quartered at the Exchange Hotel. During this time, General Sibley stayed at the hotel, "having been 'overcome' by too generous a supply of wine and brandy" at the hotel bar.[110]

One of the first acts Sibley did "was to seize all funds in the territorial treasury, which were 'appropriated either to the General's private use or for

Above: A covered wagon loaded with provisions on display at Fort Union, New Mexico. *Author's collection.*

Opposite: Ruins at Fort Union, north of Las Vegas, New Mexico, the final mustering place for the Union army before confronting the Confederate army at the Battle of Glorieta Pass. *Author's collection.*

The Story of the Old Inn at the End of the Trail

some other purpose,'" reported the *Santa Fe Gazette*. Apparently in reprisal for the newspaper's report, he seized "the keys of the printing office of the *Santa Fe Gazette*." Sibley "lingered in Santa Fe and was seen at the fandangos and dinners, quite as though he were again legitimately stationed in town."[111]

The first contingents of Sibley's army began leaving Santa Fe on April 7. Sibley left shortly thereafter. He left one hundred sick and wounded rebels behind. The *Santa Fe Gazette*, referring to Sibley's heavy drinking, reported that all the Confederates left behind were "some of Sibley's proclamations and empty champagne bottles."[112]

An interesting aftermath of the army occupation at the Exchange Hotel was the arrest of its manager, supposedly for the crime of selling liquor to Confederate soldiers. Charles G. Parker, a famous wagon master on the Santa Fe Trail, took charge of the hotel after the Rose family departed for California in 1861. His case came before the court in August after the Southern army left the city, so it may have been a case of reprisal for patronizing with the rebel army occupants. At any rate, the appropriate punishment was handed out by the court, and within a few months Charles G. Parker was back on the trail headed east after only a year's stint as hotel manager.[113] Two years later, in 1864, he came through Santa Fe at the head of a caravan headed for Chihuahua.[114]

The Soldier's Monument, dedicated to New Mexicans who died in the Mexican-American War and the Civil War, as well as wars with "Savage Indians." The structure was pulled down by demonstrators on Indigenous Day 2020. *Author's collection.*

In their arduous retreat back to Texas, the Rebels were harassed by Union troops most of the way, but they finally reached the safety of Fort Bliss, just inside the Texas border, by early May. "The Sibley Brigade was shattered and defeated, as much or more by the vastness and the sterility of the land

and by inadequate and incompetent leadership as by the Union Army," concluded Thompson. The brigade then continued on to San Antonio. "As the last of his fatigued and sore-footed soldiers limped into the streets of San Antonio in the summer of 1862, Confederate hopes for the realization of a western Manifest Destiny ceased to exist."[115]

Criticism of Sibley's performance in the New Mexico campaign plagued him for much of the rest of his life. While the general held the confidence of Jefferson Davis, his major critics were in Texas. There, the House of Representatives and the senate called for an investigation into his conduct. Because of the exigencies of the continuing war, Sibley was able to continue leading his fighting men in the lowlands of Mississippi and Louisiana. Eventually, however, his poor judgment in battle situations caught up with him, and he faced a court-martial. He was acquitted of all charges, presumably due to his connection with the president of the Confederacy.

At the close of the Civil War in the spring of 1865, Sibley moved to New York City to be with his wife and children, who had been sent there for safety with his wife's parents in the late stages of the war. After languishing there for four years, "an opportunity of a lifetime came his way. In a rare stroke of good luck he was contacted by an adventurer agent for the Khedive of Egypt." He was seeking Civil War veterans to help in reorganizing the Egyptian military. In December 1869, Sibley signed a contract to serve in Egypt for five years, with a possible five-year renewal, and he was soon on his way to Egypt.[116]

"Sibley had been one of the first Americans to arrive in Egypt, and he was also one of the first to leave." On temporary assignment in Alexandria, the general rented a luxurious apartment. The owner, an English merchant, "asserted that Sibley had not only completely wrecked the apartment but also consumed the owner's elaborate stock of alcoholic beverages." In his brief time there, he also racked up many debts and was taken to court by those to whom he was in debt. "His alcoholism…indicates beyond doubt how chronic his drinking had become. In the end it was his undoing."[117]

Dismissed by the khedive for his drunken incompetence, Sibley arrived back in New York in late 1873. He immediately traveled to Fredericksburg, Virginia, to live with his widowed daughter, Helen. He spent the rest of his days attempting to collect royalties for his Sibley Tent from the federal government. Unfortunately for Sibley Congress "passed a bill requiring that in such cases army officers would have to remain loyal to the Federal Government." Therefore, because he had joined the Confederate army, the general was not eligible to receive the royalties. He died a pauper on August 23, 1886, in Fredericksburg.[118]

11
PROSPERITY

One night a crowd of men sat, betting with intense earnestness, at a monte bank in Santa Fe. It was late, and an immense amount of silver and gold was laid upon the table. A female was dealing…and had you looked in her countenance for any symptom by which to discover how the game stood, you would have turned away unsatisfied; for calm seriousness was alone discernible, and the cards fell from her fingers as steadily as though she were handling only a knitting needle.
—*Matt Field,* On the Santa Fe Trail, *209*

The story of Santa Fe for the succeeding decades…is one of continued and increasing prosperity," wrote historian Ralph Emerson Twitchell. It was a time of new opportunities, when a man could make a name for himself. One of the locals whose star began to shine during this time was Kit Carson, the man who served as scout for the U.S. Army to California, the man who fought the Confederate rebels at Valverde. His growing fame was as the great Indian fighter of the West, as pictured romantically in American dime novels and comic books.

At the same time, Santa Fe's position as the center of military and financial activity in the Southwest caused it to become "a beneficiary from a financial, business and social viewpoint not enjoyed by any other post in the southwest." This, even as the territory lost much of its vast lands when Arizona was carved out of the western half of New Mexico in 1863. Even so, with the end of the Civil War, "there also came many men, military and civilian, accompanied by their wives and families, and Santa Fe enjoyed a brilliant social existence."[119]

The Story of the Old Inn at the End of the Trail

The Exchange Hotel, under new management, continued to be the center of social life in the city. Wagon master W.G. Parker's departure in 1862 left a vacancy in the hotel's management, and it was taken up by Hinckley, Blake & Company, the legal name of a threesome: C.S. Hinckley, C.E. Blake and D.S. Garland.[120] This management team updated the hotel interior with new furniture and improved the kitchens and parlor to meet the expectations of the new postwar society. Under their gaze, the hotel became the place where "all public social functions of an official character" were held, "and the old dining room and patio were used for the inaugural balls and ceremonies in which the military from the post always participated, lending much to the formality and unique social features of these official functions." The public rooms were lavishly decorated, and "on three sides of the patio there was a fine portal and all around were flowers and vines, and…several mocking-birds in cages."[121]

All kinds of people could be found in the hotel's main gambling hall: "officers in uniform, lieutenants, captains, majors, rubbed elbows with justices of the supreme court, civilians in every walk of life, bankers, merchants, clerks, 'cowmen'…sheep herders, governors, lawyers and politicians, with here and there a professional 'gambling man.'" The whole scene gave an air

The Fonda (Old Exchange Hotel), at the End of the Santa Fe Trail. This famous hostelry was the stopping place of many of the early settlers. Santa Fe, New Mex.

Early photograph of the Exchange Hotel. It was known as the United States Hotel for two years in the late 1840s. *1907–1910(?) Courtesy of the Palace of the Governors Photo Archives (NMHM/DCA), negative Number 016552.*

of prosperity "and gave to New Mexico's capital a reputation for hospitality and good cheer unequaled in the great southwest." At the rear of the hotel was a corral where one of the kitchens was available to those who had corral privileges: the teamsters and stagecoach drivers.[122]

An unusual sighting was reported in the *Weekly New Mexican* in late July 1864 in front of the hotel: a camel was seen lumbering down San Francisco Street. The report was brief and short on details: "We are informed, the only one remaining of those brought to the section of the country some years ago" by Lieutenant Edward F. Beale, the famous creator of the California Trail on which the Rose family traveled and turned back from the Colorado River after being attacked by the Mojave Indians in 1858. The most remarkable aspect of the entourage was that it was led by Charles G. Parker, the previous Exchange manager who was fined at the end of the war for selling liquor to soldiers.[123]

In 1865, the Exchange was purchased by Thomas McDonald and John D. Baker; they would turn out to be long-term owners, in charge of the place into the 1870s. McDonald seemed to be especially adept at hotel management, and it was he, if the glowing reports about the hotel in the *Santa Fe Gazette* are to be believed, who brought the establishment into a successful multiyear season of success. In an article about the ownership, the newspaper referred to him as "the popular genius who presides over the destinies of the Exchange Hotel." In a later article, he was lauded as one of the city's "most estimable citizens and is especially known as a thorough gentleman and an obliging host, well posted and informed in all that pertains to a 'hotel keeper,' from long practice and experience in such matters."[124]

While the city reveled in its sophistication and merchant traders from the East continued to advance Santa Fe's reputation as the commercial powerhouse of the Southwest, the obvious dissatisfaction and anger of the Native Americans was felt all around the territory. Apaches, Utes and Navajos especially were constantly on the warpath in a desperate attempt to preserve their way of life and maintain control of their lands. Kit Carson, as the preeminent wilderness champion of the West, now was an officer in the U.S. Army and under the orders of his superiors. The most urgent threat to the towns in the territory during and after the Civil War were the Navajos. Their discontent with their unhappy lot turned into violence as they increasingly attacked Spanish and American settlements in the territory.

The new commander of the army in New Mexico, General James H. Carleton, had no patience for the Native American tribes and their trepidations. He said the Navajos had long since "passed that point when talking would be of any avail. They must be whipped and fear us before they will cease killing and robbing the people."[125]

Carson was called into action. His first assignment involved moving the Mescalero Apaches from their mountain hideaways to a location called Bosque Redondo in central New Mexico, after which he was to wage a war of attrition against the Navajos. "Carleton made it clear that this precursor to the Navajo campaign was to be an all-or-nothing proposition, and he insisted that Colonel Carson wage it with ruthless efficiency." The *Mescaleros*, he said, "must be brought to their brutal senses." He also announced that all men of the tribe should be killed wherever they were found but that the women and children should be taken prisoner. "Carson was appalled by Carleton's shoot-on-sight policy and refused to obey it." Instead, he sent the leading male captives to Santa Fe to negotiate their future with the general, who then ordered all of them sent to Bosque Redondo in central New Mexico, where he envisioned a new reservation for the tribes.[126]

Dreading what he knew would be a disaster with the Navajos, and because he was not in good health, Carson decided to resign his position in the army. The letter he submitted to the general was dated February 3, 1863. The general would have none of it and demanded that his good friend and admirer stand fast. He refused Carson's resignation.[127]

Very reluctantly, Carson and a team of soldiers headed for the mountain strongholds of the Navajos along the northwestern border area where New Mexico and Arizona territorial boundaries met. He proceeded to burn their wheat and cornfields and chopped down their peach and other fruit trees in an effort to starve the Indians. They were given a deadline of August 1863 to surrender to the U.S. Army. Those who surrendered were forced to march to Fort Canby in eastern Arizona, later to be removed to the site of Bosque Redondo on the Pecos River, nearly four hundred miles to the east. Carleton's purpose was to move them to this new location, "there to feed and take care of them until they have opened farms and become able to support themselves, as the Pueblo Indians of New Mexico are doing."[128]

Carleton's plan "would thus require a forced relocation on a scale not undertaken since the 1830s, when the Cherokee of the Southeastern United States were made to embark on their bitter Trail of Tears exodus to Oklahoma," says author Hampton Sides in his treatise on the subject. He suggests Carleton should have known better, based on past battles with the Navajos. "Through the ages, battling the Navajos had consistently shown itself to be tricky and ultimately unsatisfying work." Now it would cast a shadow of culpability on underling Kit Carson that would be a blemish on his name for ages to come.[129]

The Long Walk from Fort Canby took several routes, the two major ones being the "Santa Fe Route" and the "Mountain Route." The Santa Fe Route followed the Rio Grande north from Albuquerque along the Camino Real, the Royal Road, past the pueblos of Sandia, San Felipe and Santo Domingo. It then veered along a stream to Santa Fe and followed the Santa Fe Trail out to the Pecos River. Little is recorded about the march through Santa Fe or its passing the Exchange Hotel. One can imagine the pitiful site to the city's business class as the bedraggled lines of somber Indians from this proud tribe struggled to keep up the pace. Many of their children were stolen along the trail and taken away to be slaves when parents were too sick to watch over them. Many of all ages died along the wayside. It must have been the most pitiful parade ever seen in the city.[130]

A major portion of the tribe finally arrived at Bosque Redondo. At first glance, they thought it was a beautiful place, but that impression quickly faded as they set about preparing the land for cultivation. By tool and by hand, they immediately began work on irrigation ditches and channels to divert water from the river's main flow. All too soon they discovered that the water was not fit to drink or even to water plants; it was alkaline and only made people sick. Additionally, they could not abide the Apaches who were already there. Carleton's plan was a disaster.

News of the disastrous situation came to the attention of the federal government. "Between 1865 and 1868…the Executive Branch investigated. Congress investigated. The Department of the Interior investigated. The Army investigated." They all concluded that it was an appalling situation. Carleton was relieved of duty in New Mexico in 1866 and was assigned to a post in Louisiana. In the spring of 1868, General William T. Sherman visited Fort Sumner near Bosque Redondo and interviewed their chief, Barboncito, and other tribal leaders. He was deeply moved by their plight and agreed that they should be permitted to return to their homeland. "Further, he promised that America would give the Navajos seed stock and tools to help them get a new start in life, and America would help liberate their children from slavery. This time, America kept its promise."[131]

As the Navajos returned to their homeland and began starting life all over again, Carson was back in his hometown, Taos, having just returned from Washington, D.C. His travel to the capital was in the company of Ute chiefs, who paid a visit to the president. While there, Carson was evaluated by medical specialists for his ailments. He was diagnosed with an "aneurism of the aorta, in addition to being a constant sufferer from a bronchial affection. It was only a matter of time and his career would close." His wife died in April 1868, leaving seven children. The end came for Carson in late May, when he was "visiting one of his sons at Ft. Lyon, Colorado. General Carson attempted to mount a horse, resulting in a fatal hemorrhage—a ruptured artery in the neck." A doctor was summoned, but medical attention by then was useless. "His life quietly ebbed away. A brief struggle, three gasping words: 'Doctor, compadre, adios,' and his brave soul had fled."[132]

12
INCIDENT AT THE EXCHANGE

How changed the earth! Yet heaven is the same.
Those are the stars which smiled upon me when
A hundred leagues away I heard my name
Spoken by brothers in the haunts of men.
And shall those brothers greet me e'er again?
Ye silent stars, my sole companions now,
For once reveal yourselves to mortal ken.
And here your solemn mysteries avow.
Why does man turn to thee when gloom is on his brow?
—Matt Field, On the Santa Fe Trail, *287*

It was probably a somewhat pleasant winter day in December 1867. Only two weeks until Christmas, and anticipation was building for the joyous holiday. Buildings on the Santa Fe Plaza were decorated with boughs of evergreens and southwestern holly, the variety that produces blue berries instead of red. Blue skies prevail in New Mexico even on the coldest days, when daylight temperatures usually range between forty and sixty degrees in Santa Fe. It had been only seven years since the Confederate invasion of the city. People were optimistic, and business was booming. In the previous year, nearly six thousand wagons had arrived in the city, and more were expected this year.

General Robert B. Mitchell was the new governor, appointed by President Andrew Johnson just one year earlier. Local and state government was functioning, and the territorial legislature was sitting for its yearly session.

State representatives and senators were in juxtaposition for their causes and leadership positions.

Among them was Lieutenant Colonel William Logan Rynerson from Doña Ana County in the south. A military veteran, he served in the army under General Carleton and was mustered out in 1866. As a war hero, at age thirty-nine he was a prime candidate for a seat in the legislature. He had a Democratic opponent who was declared victor in the election. However, soon after a vote recount, Secretary of the Territory Herman H. Heath declared that the winner's certificate was fraudulent. Rynerson was declared the rightful victor. When the upper chamber commenced its opening ceremonies on December 2, he was the only Republican and the only Anglo senator.[133]

It was a customary, time-honored tradition that the territorial supreme court justice administer the oath of office to new members of the legislature. At this time, General John P. Slough, also a war veteran, was chief justice. He was also thirty-nine years of age and had years of experience in legal affairs in Ohio, Kansas and Colorado before being posted by the president to New Mexico. He was well known in the territory because of his decisive action at thwarting the advance to the north by the Confederate army in 1862. He was organizer and commander of the Colorado volunteer Federal army that came south to challenge the Confederates in what turned out to be the Battle of Glorieta Pass.[134]

Both men had friends in leadership of their parties; Rynerson had a good friend in territorial Secretary H.H. Heath. Slough was offended when the Republican-led legislature invited Heath to administer the oath of office to the new legislators in 1867. It was customary for out-of-town legislators to find relief from lawmaking of the day by returning in the evening to their lodgings at the Exchange and to relax in the amusements and games that were on offer there. In the billiard room of the hotel one night, Slough was heard to call Rynerson a thief and a coward who had stolen both in and out of the army, including his present seat in the legislature.[135]

The slur was passed on to the senator by the person to whom Slough gave his comments. The next day, December 14, the legislature passed a resolution against the judge, introduced by Rynerson, that was "derogatory to his official conduct and private character." The action was passed by the legislature and charged the chief justice of "being unsupportably unjust; with improperly imprisoning and fining jurors; with being governed by political and party prejudices." He was also accused of having an "ungovernable temper." Most importantly, the resolution concluded with a petition asking for his removal from office by the president.[136]

On the fifteenth, Rynerson returned to the hotel at midday with a concealed Colt revolver and paced back and forth in front of the billiard room awaiting the judge's appearance. "As soon as he saw the judge, he presented his pistol and demanded a retraction of the language that had been used the evening previous." The judge refused to make the retraction, and Rynerson immediately fired, "the ball taking effect in the lower portion of the abdomen, passing into the intestines, and inflicted a mortal wound."[137]

At a hearing about the matter that took place shortly after the event, the "judge remanded the prisoner to jail without setting bond. Several days later, Rynerson demanded a writ of habeas corpus, and on January 23, 1868, Judge Perry Brocchus released Rynerson on a twenty-thousand-dollar bond." The liberated senator returned to the legislative hall, where the lawmaking season was still in progress. He was immediately cast into the final days of a tumultuous political fray.

"Rynerson was eventually tried in March for Slough's murder and was acquitted by the jury on a plea of self-defense." A witness of the shooting clinched the jury's decision when he testified that as the shot was fired and Slough began to fall, he saw a Derringer pistol clatter to the floor from Slough's pocket.[138]

Rynerson continued to be a force in New Mexican politics and business as a senator and as a major landholder in the Doña Ana County area. "William L. Rynerson, who entered New Mexico in 1862 as a California Volunteer, became one of southern New Mexico's outstanding political and civic leaders.…He was a typical example of the booster-businessman who controlled western politics." He died on September 26, 1893.[139] In his later years, he had become a magistrate, during which he had to deal with one of the most famous gunslingers in history.

That gunslinger came to Santa Fe as a boy with his mother, little brother and his mother's suitor in late 1872. Traveling by wagon or stage, the foursome was deposited at the Exchange Hotel at the end of the trail they had followed from Colorado by way of the Raton Pass. Catherine McCarty was mother of Joseph and William. Her suitor was William Antrim, whom she married at the First Presbyterian Church of Santa Fe on March 1, 1863.

After the marriage, the family reportedly moved into the Exchange, where young William, age twelve, did odd jobs such as a busboy in the restaurant, a dishwasher and a messenger. He learned Spanish and how to play cards, talents he would use through life to become the famous Billy the Kid.[140]

Another war veteran who made his home at the Exchange was Captain John Martin. Like Rynerson, he had joined the California Column under

The Story of the Old Inn at the End of the Trail

Billy the Kid. *Courtesy of the Palace of the Governors Photo Archives (NMHM/DCA), negative Number 030769.*

General Carleton and marched from the coast to the Rio Grande at the time of the Civil War. He married Esther Catherine Wadsworth in 1865, and they went to live first near Fort Seldon, where he built and conducted a ferryboat at the regional river crossing. At the fort, his wife got a job as manager of the officer's mess.

His real claim to fame came when he made his next move, to the Jornada del Muerto ("Route of the Dead Man"), a one-hundred-mile desert section of the Royal Road connecting Santa Fe and Mexico City. It was the most remote and arid zone of the whole route through old or New Mexico, where water was not to be found. Nevertheless, Martin suspected there might be underground water if one could sink a well. He knew the Jornada well; during his army duties, he was charged with escorting mail wagons between Las Cruces and Santa Fe. He moved his family out to the middle of the trail and began digging. He dug to a depth of 164 feet before finding water.

In the dry desert, the discovery of water was a bonanza. Martin built a horse and cattle ranch and stage stop known as the Aleman Ranch, where his six children learned how to do hard work. During their eight years operating the ranch and accommodating stage drivers and passengers, they accumulated considerable wealth and, in 1875, decided they would like to experience city life. The Martins heard about a hotel in Santa Fe that was for sale. They headed for the capital city and purchased the Exchange.[141]

They arrived in the midst of celebrations throughout the city as the town was honoring Bishop Jean-Baptiste Lamy's ascension to the rank of archbishop. His appointment had been declared earlier in the year by the pope, but official ceremonies were not organized until summer. The largest procession the city had yet seen was launched from the church at the east end of San Francisco Street, passed the Exchange and continued up the Santa Fe Trail to St. Michael's College, where the official events culminated.

The Martins soon were established at their hotel and began receiving accolades. A local newspaper lavished praise on the new hotel owners. "This hotel is winning golden opinions….Guests…prefer a first-class house to any other." Esther Martin was especially praised. "Its cuisine is under the personal supervision of Mrs. Martin and superintended by perhaps as good a steward as can be found in western country." Without being specific, the report said, "There has been an improvement in everything about the Exchange." It concluded that Santa Fe was glad that "this city has at last secured a first-class Hotel."[142]

In 1876, another event caught the attention of people in the city. "Some excitement was created near the Exchange Hotel....A teamster in Government employ named Geo. Blaugh" was among a detachment of troops headed out the Santa Fe Trail. When he got to the hotel, he refused to go any farther. The officer in charge ordered him tied to the wagon, but Blaugh "appealed to the citizens present stating that he was not an enlisted man. A sheriff's deputy was called who released him."[143]

The story seems of little significance, except that the report concluded that the man in question, Blaugh, was a "colored man." It seems to be one of the earliest reports of the presence of Black military men being deployed to the West at this time to take on the marauding Indians in the territory. This was also when the Native Americans started referring to the Black army soldiers as "Buffalo Soldiers," because they saw a similarity of their hair with the black mane of the buffalo that roamed the plains. "Men of the Tenth, and later the Ninth, accepted the title and wore it proudly." Indeed, a main feature of the regimental crest of the Tenth Cavalry featured a buffalo.[144]

At the hotel, the rooms were full and the kitchens, under the supervision of Esther Martin, were working overtime to meet demands. "To accommodate all the wants of the public...meals can be had at all hours from 6 o'clock in the morning until 12 at night." The quality of food was said to have reached heights never before seen in Santa Fe. The menu for New Year's dinner of 1877, for example, offered three soups, ten meats and fish, seven entrées, thirteen vegetables, eight relishes, five pies, three puddings and five desserts. And "everything was served up in excellent style under direction of the steward Mr. Frank Martin."[145]

The pressure of management began to take a toll on the exceptional team in charge, the Martins. Some months into the New Year, a tragedy came upon the family. John Martin retired to a room at the front of the hotel, where he had a comfortable chair and chatted with friends for a few moments. Then "while quietly sitting in a chair smoking, as was his usual after dinner custom, he was seen to be...suddenly convulsed and gasping for breath." A doctor who lived nearby was called immediately, but "before the doctor could reach him, Mr. Martin breathed his last."[146]

13
END OF THE TRAIL

Now they are bridging o'er the stream
To pass across each loaded team
Throwing in heavy brush and grass
To bear the wagons as they pass,
To keep the skittish mules from falling
And guard the sinking wheels from stalling.
And Double teams they still require
To drag the Waggons [sic] *through the mire.*
Behold with what a fearful pitch
The lumbering wagon jumps the ditch.
See how the frightened mules are staring
Hear the whips crack, and Drivers swearing.
—*Matt Field,* On the Santa Fe Trail, *7*

Former sailor, soldier and Indian agent John Ayers served as administrator of the Exchange after his friend John Martin passed away. He immediately began searching for a new owner by placing an ad in local newspapers: "Hotel Men: Owing to the recent death of the proprietor of the Exchange Hotel…an unusually good opportunity is offered…to take and keep the only first-class Hotel in this city."[147]

The newspaper soon announced that a woman, not a man, Mrs. S.B. Davis from nearby Las Vegas, was the new proprietress of the hotel. The report stated that under the supervision of Mrs. Davis, the hotel has been "rejuvenated and improved." It also encouraged customers, "All the features that have so signally contributed to its extensive reputation will be maintained and everything done to add to the comfort of guests." Lest the public worry about the good eats, "The Hotel Table will be under the control of Cooks of the Highest Grade, and meals will be served in the best style."[148]

The new hotel proprietress was installed none too soon, because several important visitors were about to descend on the city. Additionally, several new hotels were close to opening their doors, bringing more competition for the aging Exchange.

The first notables were the new territorial governor, General Lew Wallace, and his wife, Susan. "At nine o'clock in the evening of September 29, 1878, a horse-drawn carriage clattered to a stop in front of the La Fonda hotel in Santa Fe....Lew Wallace...stepped off the carriage and surveyed the narrow streets and the nearby mountains that loomed over the city."[149]

General Lew Wallace, governor of New Mexico from 1878 to 1881. *Engraving after a photograph by Napoleon Sarony. Courtesy of the Palace of the Governors Photo Archives (NMHM/DCA), negative Number 013123.*

"We reach the open Plaza," Susan described her arrival. "Long one-story adobe houses front it on every side. And this is the historic city! Older than our government, older than the Spanish Conquest, it looks older than the hills surrounding it, and worn-out besides." She tended to dramatize her writing. "'*El Fonda!*' shouts the driver, as we stop before the hotel." Most Spanish speakers still referred to the Exchange as the *fonda*, and the term was taken up by many of the people who referred to it fondly in this way.[150]

On his second day, the new governor went to the Palace of the Governors in the Plaza to "inform Samuel B. Axtell, a former San Francisco lawyer and congressman, that he was being replaced as governor." The Santa Fe political machine that had developed in recent years, known as the Santa Fe Ring, controlled much of the trade that went on in the territory. Axtell lost his job as a result of his association with the group when newcomers came trying to make their fortune and found the territory divided up and controlled by members of the Ring. News about controlling acts of the Ring floated back to the federal government.

Probably the most notable contest between the Ring and newcomers was taking place south of Santa Fe in Lincoln County, where two factions were at such odds that the situation was called the "Lincoln County War." Billy the Kid was a major actor in the street gunfights that were taking place almost on a daily basis in the war-torn county. Numerous people were already dead due to the frequent shoot-outs, including the sheriff at one point. "Alarmed by the violence and rumors that Governor Axtell's administration had been filled with 'corruption, fraud, mismanagement, plots and murder,' federal officials had turned to Wallace to bring peace to the region."[151]

That night, as the governor returned to his lodgings at the Exchange, he began developing his strategy for dealing with the Lincoln County War. He would determine who was responsible for the offences, offer a pardon to the perpetrators and even travel down to Lincoln to sort things out himself if necessary. Unfortunately, it would take over a year to completely see a cessation of hostilities. Meanwhile, Wallace would enjoy the hospitality at the hotel until Axtell could vacate his offices in the Palace on the other side of the Plaza.

"Attorneys at Santa Fe were retained by the factions involved in the Lincoln County troubles." They would cause the governor no end of trials and lead him to declare, in the end, that all strategies used elsewhere were to no avail in New Mexico. He found solace from his daily struggles by secluding himself in his office at night and, with a candle on his desk, write, write, write. His wife did similarly, and each would end up at the end of their sojourn in Santa Fe with a published book to their name.[152]

In this manner, time passed quickly for the state's top executive. In just over a year's time, one of the most exciting events in Santa Fe's history occurred: the train tracks arrived, an event that would drastically change the trajectory of the city and the territory. For the first time, a sitting president would visit, and one of the most notorious gunslingers in the West would take up residence in the Santa Fe jail.

The Exchange became the scene of a devastating event in mid-1878 that shocked the citizenry. A young man by the name of Jean B. Lamy, nephew to the archbishop, had arrived about nine years previous. He became known as J.B. Lamy, to distinguish himself from his famous uncle. Soon, J.B. met and fell in love with a young Santa Fe beauty by the name of Doña Mercedes Chávez. Daughter of former governor José Chaves, she was a popular socialite in town. She and J.B. soon married and were able to obtain a fine house in lower San Francisco Street. They furnished the house with elegant furniture, and Mercedes enjoyed hosting guests at large parties there.

Several months later, a young French architect arrived to help with the planning of a new cathedral for the city; his name was François Mallet. He became a good friend of the young Lamy couple. When they traveled in their handsome carriage around town, Mallet was often with them. He greatly enjoyed the hospitality of their home.

Soon, rumors were being whispered in town that the architect was courting Mercedes Lamy. She became unhappy at home and often quarreled with her husband. Because of her change in attitude, J.B. suspected that Mallet was the cause. Mercedes left home and found private lodgings. She obtained the services of an attorney and filed for divorce. Mercedes soon was seen strolling in town on the arm of Mallet and was seen being escorted by him to social events.[153]

Her former husband became ill with anxiety over the situation and nearly had a nervous breakdown. He hoped for reconciliation with his former wife, but her parading around town with Mallet was more than he could bear. In early September, the two young men were enjoying the entertainments on offer at the Exchange. Overwhelmed by emotion, J.B. pulled out a concealed pistol and shot Mallet from behind when he was at the hotel entrance. Mallet died immediately. J.B. surrendered to two lawmen and was arrested.

At the ensuing trial, a prominent doctor from the Kansas State Medical Association, D.D. Farley, testified to the unstable mental condition of Lamy at the time of the shooting. The jury, after several attempts to reach a verdict, finally acquitted the murderer by reason of temporary insanity. Surprisingly, in time, the young couple reconciled and spent the rest of their lives together.[154]

In early February 1880, the city was bursting with anticipation. The first train of the Atchison, Topeka and Santa Fe Railway was to arrive on its maiden entrance to the capital city. As state and local officials assembled amid an immense crowd to witness the event, the last spike was driven at high noon on Monday, February 9. A parade assembled on the west side of the Santa Fe Plaza.

The state marshal, on horseback, was in the lead, followed by the Ninth Cavalry Band and territorial, county and federal officials. At the depot, students from city schools lined the platform, and two bands were stationed on either side of the platform. Governor Wallace was among the officiating party. Chief Justice L. Bradford Prince gave a glowing speech heralding the long-awaited event.

The people marveled at this incredible ceremony—the anticipation was now reality. Only a dozen years before, people making the journey by stage

The Atchison, Topeka & Santa Fe engine known as "Baby" arrived at Santa Fe in early 1880. *Photograph by Ben Wittick. Courtesy of the Palace of the Governors Photo Archives (NMHM/DCA), negative Number 015780.*

from Missouri endured two weeks of discomfort, had miserable meals at irregular intervals and arrived exhausted in Santa Fe. Before stagecoach service, covered wagons took over two months to accomplish the task. The newspaper quipped that a person on such a trip "once arrived at Santa Fe was almost willing to spend the remainder of his life here rather than go through the same experience the second time."[155]

The increased flow of people from the East on the train would test the accommodations of the city. The continued success of the Exchange would now depend on its old-world charm, its service and excellent food, because the new glimmering hotel, the Palace, just a few blocks away, was the cause of much excitement. Another hotel, Herlow's, had also recently opened farther west on San Francisco Street.

For the first time, a hotel reviewer visited the city and cited the pros and cons of the three establishments. He found the Palace to be quite glamorous with its newly installed gas lamps and noted that the Herlow was popular with miners.

The Exchange, however, "impresses the visitor, upon getting an outside view, as being the last place to find good hotel accommodations, but the impression is at once dispelled upon entering." Once through the door, the reviewer was smitten by "an exceedingly comfortable office which contains a large old-fashioned fire-place, in which a roaring fire of logs supplies warmth and a jolly cheerful light, making you feel at home and your departure a season of regret."

Furthermore, "they have refurnished the Exchange in excellent style and with good taste, and are setting a most excellent table, are doing a prosperous and profitable business, and they deserve all they get in the way of patronage, for they are mighty nice hospitable gentlemen whom it is a pleasure to know." The new proprietors were Reed and Bishop, having succeeded Mrs. S.B. Davis, who left for the new Plaza Hotel in Las Vegas, the last train stop before Santa Fe.[156]

In all the excitement about the train arrival, most of Santa Fe never gave a thought to the fate of the Santa Fe Trail—or the Exchange Hotel. As for the Santa Fe Trail, it immediately became history. No longer would the crack of whips echo across the landscape. As for the hotel, it would struggle on for a few more years.

14

A FESTIVE EXCHANGE

> *Beauty and repose are attributes of evening in any clime; but here, at the mountain's foot, when the sun is hid beyond the tall peaks above, and a thin grey shadow falls over Santa Fe; while the blue sky is still illuminated with slanting sun-beams, and floating clouds are bathed in golden radiance; here, in the little mud-built Mexican town, beauty and repose seem folded away from the world, like flowers smiling in the desert, like young genius shrinking from the very admiration for which it pants in secret.*
> —Matt Field, On the Santa Fe Trail, 235

If the first half of 1880 was exciting, the second half was equally so, not only for the people of Santa Fe but also for the Exchange Hotel. The Santa Fe Trail was now silent except for local short trips at various points; the trail to Santa Fe now featured iron tracks that glistened in the sun and stretched to the horizon. The rails were the harbinger of hordes of new people descending on Santa Fe; several notable ones were about to arrive in the city during the last half of this year. As for the old Exchange Hotel, events were to take place that seemed like a last hurrah for a building that had played such a vital role in the development of the West.

Casual observers would never have guessed it, but the territorial governor, Lew Wallace, had a secret hobby that sustained him during the turbulent days of the booming capital city and the territory of New Mexico. During the day, he was a dutiful official tending to Indian Wars, military matters, the Lincoln County War and daily duties of his office. But at night, he was a recluse. He hid in a small room of the Palace of the Governors to take up his pen and continue work on his book.

His evenings in the little room next to his office became "a perfect retreat from the annoyances of daily life as they are spun for me by enemies, and friends who might as well be enemies," he said. "When I reach the words 'The End' how beautiful they will look to me," he wrote. The book was seven years in the making, research taking the bulk of that time. But it was in that little dark room where his writing brilliance found light. At last, in March, he completed the final draft of the manuscript of *Ben Hur*, written in purple ink to honor the Easter season. He was pleased with the results and now could plan to take it to the editor in New York.

Just before he was to ship his manuscript, the mayor's wife, Flora Spiegelberg, happened to pass by his office. "I looked into the window and the Governor beckoned to me to come in. He said: 'I have just wrapped up my manuscript of *Ben Hur* to forward to my publishers. Do you think it is worth the expressage [postage]?'"

For a moment, she stared at him and then replied, "I will gladly pay half of the expressage if you agree to divide the royalties with me!"

"I will consider your offer," he chuckled.

Some years later, she wrote that his royalties amounted to nearly $1 million. "I often joked with him about my offer and how wise he was not to have accepted it."[157]

In New York, he presented the manuscript to Joseph Henry Harper of Harper & Brothers. "This is the most beautiful manuscript that has ever come into this house," effused Harper. "A bold experiment to make Christ a hero that has been often tried and always failed."[158]

While Wallace was in New York, preparations were underway in Santa Fe for the visit of another general, one of the most famous at the time: Ulysses S. Grant, the former president. A newspaper editorial fussed about the town's condition and its readiness to receive such royalty. It said of the Plaza, "The quantity of filth and fertilizing substances which overspread the Plaza grounds suggests that it could be changed into a cabbage garden!"[159]

Sketch of General Ulysses S. Grant, former president of the United States. *Clipart courtesy of FCIT (https://etc.usf.edu/clipart).*

In June, the great man arrived. "Long before the hour when the iron horse that drew the iron-hearted commander triumphantly into the city had arrived, thousands of people assembled at the depot to greet the incoming train," reported the *Santa Fe New Mexican*. When the general alighted from the train, a welcome speech was given by city leader T.B. Catron. "This duty is peculiarly pleasant to us, from the fact that you are the first of all men who, having held the high office of chief executive of any nation, has ever set foot upon the soil of New Mexico," he said.

The general gave a brief response, and 'the visitors were then shown to their carriages and conveyed to the Plaza. General Grant rode in a carriage drawn by four white horses, preceded by the band of the 13th Infantry." A reception and further celebrations continued at the Palace of the Governors.[160]

Grant was elected president of the San Pedro and Canyon del Agua Mining Company, which touted capital of $10,000. Stocks in the company jumped from $2 to $375, and Grant's annual salary was set at $25,000. Festivities surrounding his lengthy visit continued for a couple of weeks, including a ball and a banquet at the Exchange, according to historian Twitchell.[161]

It was announced that President, Rutherford B. Hayes, Secretary of War Alexander Ramsay and General William Tecumseh Sherman would be visiting in October. The planners for this event were at odds about what type of entertainment would be appropriate for the president. He was known as a "temperance man," and some felt a banquet "would be a tame affair without wines, and it would not be just the thing to invite the president to an entertainment at which they were served."

The presidential party was returning east by wagon following a trip to California. They arrived in late October, escorted by Santa Fe military. Welcoming ceremonies took place on the Plaza, across from the Exchange Hotel. The Ninth Cavalry Band performed for the president and his wife, Lucy. However, they would not overnight at the hotel: Mayor Lehman Spiegelberg and his wife, Flora, decided that, "as there were no first-class hotels in Santa Fe," their new home would be more comfortable for the president's party.

"It was one of the greatest holidays Santa Fe ever knew," Flora declared. "And when the President and his wife returned to Washington, they sent us tokens of appreciation…their autographed pictures and invited all of us to visit them, as their guests at the White House." While the president did not overnight at the Exchange, it is believed that one or two of the celebrity events during the president's stay were hosted at the hotel.[162]

Left: Sketch of President Rutherford B. Hayes. *Clipart courtesy of FCIT (https://etc.usf. edu/clipart).*

Right: Willi Spiegelberg, mayor of Santa Fe in the early 1880s. *Courtesy of the Palace of the Governors Photo Archives (NMHM/DCA) negative 050486.*

General Sherman, addressing the assemblage on one occasion, said, "You must improve your land…or the new race will come in here and displace you…and get rid of your burros and goats. I hope ten years hence there won't be any adobe houses in the territory."[163]

Another notable party arrived two days after Christmas. Sheriff Pat Garrett of Lincoln County and his posse arrived on the evening train from Las Vegas. They had with them, in shackles, Billy the Kid and two of his outlaw friends. The train was greatly delayed; that wasn't uncommon, but the late-evening arrival was caused by an incident in Las Vegas. The local sheriff there was demanding that one of Billy's friends by the name of Rudabaugh be held in the Las Vegas jail; he was accused of murdering a local law officer some months previous. Sheriff Garrett threatened to shoot anyone who attempted to take the culprit by force, so the train was permitted to leave for Santa Fe.[164]

Governor Wallace had issued several statements in local papers promising a reward for Billy's capture. "I will pay $500 reward to any person or persons who will capture William Bonny, alias The Kid, and deliver him to any sheriff of New Mexico," read the notice.[165]

Sheriff Garrett, as the one who finally apprehended Billy, at a place known as Stinking Springs on the edge of the Taiban stream in Lincoln County, was due to receive the $500 reward. In the end, it was several months before the territorial legislature voted to approve the expenditure. In the meantime, Garrett received an estimated $7,000 from citizens relieved that he had brought in the notorious gunman of the Lincoln County War.

The Exchange Hotel would not be the domicile for these characters; they were headed to jail. The new Santa Fe jail was apparently full of inmates when the entourage arrived on the evening of December 27, so it is conjectured that the prisoners were temporarily housed in the stone basement of the old jail on San Francisco Street and moved shortly thereafter to the new county jail, made of adobe mud bricks, on Water Street. The newspaper reported that they were "shut up in a stone cell to which even the light of day is denied admittance."[166]

Billy remained in the Santa Fe jail for several months and then was sent south to be tried for murder. He was convicted and sentenced to death by hanging. After another daring escape, he was finally tracked down by Garrett, who shot him on a dark night in Lincoln County.

Another interesting character who alighted from a train during this year from Missouri was a man who would become renowned as an anthropologist. His name was Adolph Bandelier. He came to study the life and times of the Native American Pueblo tribes of New Mexico. His first excavations took place at Pecos on the Santa Fe Trail and then the pueblos of Santo Domingo and Cochiti south of Santa Fe.[167]

The incredible year, 1880, closed with its multiple memorable events: the arrival of the railroad; the capture of Billy the Kid; the visit of the president; the publishing of Wallace's book, *Ben Hur*; and the quiet demise of the Santa Fe Trail as one of the great roads of early America. The Exchange, instead of being at the hub of tourist activity, became a distant competitor to the tourist boom caused by the arrival of the trains at the Santa Fe Depot located a half mile southwest of the Plaza.

15
RESURRECTION

Night now was closing rapidly…and in the eastern sky the stars came peeping out, bathing brighter radiance as the golden flood of light sank fading behind the mountains. The vast prairies were folded away in a heavy mantle of gloom, tinkling bells were heard no more, a crescent moon came smiling from the far horizon, and starry night succeeded. Santa Fe never slept beneath a lovelier night, and night never followed a more beautiful evening.
—*Matt Field,* On the Santa Fe Trail, *237*

The Exchange was sold to Dr. Robert Longwell and Abraham Staab in 1881. The previous proprietress, Mrs. S.B. Davis, had decided to return to nearby Las Vegas to manage the Plaza Hotel there. Under her supervision, "the last glorious days of the Exchange ran their course." By this time, "the Exchange had become very rundown and dilapidated."[168]

The new owners had an inspired innovation for a new way to use the building for potential profit. "A successful merchant and landholder, Staab upgraded the property by adding retail shops on San Francisco Street and renovating the original building." It would change the focus of the property from being solely a hotel to becoming a hub for a variety of retail shops.[169]

The new owners, apparently backed by a consortium of merchants in Santa Fe, represented by Longwell and Staab, realized that the upgrade to the old hotel was desperately needed if it was to compete. Together they raised $10,000 for the project. Santa Fe now had other, newer hotels: Harlow's, the Grand Central, the Palace. "Mr. J.B. Randell, of the firm Wheeler &

The Story of the Old Inn at the End of the Trail

Randell architects, was engaged yesterday in preparing the plans for the Exchange hotel, showing what the building will be when the extensive improvements…have been made."

The new owners, especially Staab, were determined to revive the old building. "The idea now is to so change the property as to make it vie with if not surpass all other hotels in the city." Plans called for enlargement of the dining room, a remodel of the entrance office and even addition of a second story over some sections. Work on the upgrades was to begin immediately, and "the new year will therefore find the Exchange Hotel a very different place."[170]

Abraham Staab was born in Paderborn, Westphalia, Germany, on February 27, 1839. "He became one of the wealthiest and most influential men in the American Southwest,"

Businessman Abraham Staab, longtime partner-owner of the Exchange Hotel. *Courtesy of the Palace of the Governors Photo Archives (NMHM/DCA) negative 011040.*

according to his gravestone epitaph.[171] At fifteen years of age, he "embarked for the United States in a sailing vessel, the voyage consuming five weeks." He found a job in Norfolk, Virginia, "as an errand boy in a small grocery store, with a salary of one dollar per week, his board and lodging included." At one of the shops where he frequently delivered packages, the merchant "took a fancy to the young apprentice, gave him employment at three dollars a week and during the evening hours gave him instruction in bookkeeping."[172]

He heard of great opportunities in the West to make his fortune as a retailer in Santa Fe, where there was a small but growing community of Jewish merchants. Shortly after the end of the Civil War, Staab became a U.S. citizen on July 10, 1865. According to a descendant, Hannah Nordhaus, who studied his life and that of his wife, Julia, Staab "promptly departed for Germany in search of a bride. My great-great-grandparents married on Christmas Day, 1865. Julia was 21 years old, Abraham 26."[173]

They boarded a ship headed to New York City, the RMS *Scotia*, in the dead of winter, January 1866. Winter followed them on the train to the American Midwest and across the prairies by stagecoach to Santa Fe. The young bride had little information about where she was going with her new husband, and they arrived in Santa Fe while it was still winter in 1866. She couldn't speak English or Spanish.

Julia must have been appalled at conditions in Santa Fe and their first lodgings. One historian asserts that they first lived in an adobe house in Burro Alley, the road where stables were kept for the many burros that carried needed firewood about the city. "Most of these dwellings traditionally housed notorious gambling dens."[174]

But Abraham promised to build her a mansion. In addition to his general store on the Plaza, Staab became a real estate tycoon with investments throughout the New Mexico Territory. "With the arrival of the railroad, interest in Santa Fe real estate soared. Land speculators contemplated new large-scale developments around the city." Staab invested heavily in a residential development plot around the new railroad depot at the western edge of the city. He was one of those who "promoted these lots as excellent investments for commercial or residential use." A New York real estate promoter was hired to auction off the lots. "Complimentary carriage rides from the Plaza and a heavily advertised free lunch promoted both auctions. Every lot sold."[175]

In a few years, Abraham did build a mansion for his bride. "The Victorian mansion was completed in 1882, and she loved to decorate it with fresh roses.…The house was also perfect for entertaining, and she instantly became the social queen of society." She was the perfect hostess, "but she was also a devoted mother to her seven children." But the fairytale life did not last. "When an eighth child, a daughter named Henriette, died in 1883, just a few weeks after her birth, Julia sank into deep depression. Distraught with grief, she neither ate nor slept for two weeks." She became a recluse. "When she finally emerged, her formerly beautiful raven hair had turned white. She was never the same after that."[176]

Even though Staab was not a magistrate in the city, his status as a leading citizen and major entrepreneur did not protect him from several encounters with gunslingers of the Wild West. One notable event occurred when he was traveling with a colleague and two Sisters of Charity on a return trip to Santa Fe from Trinidad, Colorado. Sister Blandina Segale had agreed to accompany Mr. and Mrs. Staab and the children to the railhead at that town, in late 1877. Segale was manager of the city's first hospital, Saint Vincent's.

It was known that Billy the Kid was operating as a robber along the Santa Fe Trail around Las Vegas at the time. Their wagon called at a stage stop called Sweetwater, and they noticed the waiting stage driver and his passengers were already at the building, "loading or cleaning revolvers and rifles.…We were told that 'Billy's gang was dodging around and we expect they will attack us tonight.'" Early the next morning, Sister Blandina's party climbed into their carriage and headed south on the trail to Santa Fe.

They hadn't gone far when suddenly word came from the driver that a horseback rider was seen in the distance headed in their direction. "Instantly each man took out his revolver." Soon the driver said, "He am very near." Sister Blandina recorded, "I looked at the men and could not but admire the resolute expression which meant 'To conquer or die.'"

What the men did not understand was that Blandina had a special relationship with Billy that traced back to their first encounter when she was serving in Trinidad several years before. She had discovered that a wounded friend of his was languishing in a small house in town. At that time, Billy promised her that he would respect her wishes in appreciation of her care for his friend.

Sister Blandina Segale of the Sisters of Charity Order, 1870–80. *Courtesy of the Palace of the Governors Photo Archives (NMHM/DCA) negative 067735.*

Now she urged the men, "If the comer is a scout from the gang, our chance is in remaining passive. I would suggest putting revolvers out of sight."

Again the driver shouted, "He am very near."

"The light patter of hoofs could be heard as they drew near the carriage….I shifted my big bonnet so that when he did look, he could see the Sisters. Our eyes met; he raised his large-brimmed hat with a wave and a bow…then stopped to give us some of his wonderful antics on bronco maneuvers. The rider was the famous Billy the Kid!"

If Staab had his brushes with death, his partner in the hotel business, Longwell, had even more. Robert Hamilton Longwell was born on April 20, 1840, in Gettysburg, Pennsylvania. As a young man, he became interested in studying medicine and was accepted at the Jefferson Medical College in Philadelphia. After graduating in 1863, he served as a civilian doctor in the U.S. Army at Mowrer General Hospital in that city, where he treated wounded casualties during the Civil War.[177]

He was then posted to Fort Wingate, New Mexico, for two years, then transferred to Fort Union. He returned to Pennsylvania, where he married Elizabeth Kenney in 1871. They moved to New Mexico, where he was put in charge of the Cimarron Agency by the U.S. Department of Indian

Affairs. It was during this time that he became involved in land speculation in a scheme that became known as the "Colfax County War."

Cimarron was the scene of many arguments and gunfights as two factions contended for land in the Maxwell Land Grant, the largest piece of disputed land in the United States. Longwell sided with the group of leaders in Santa Fe, the Santa Fe Ring. His involvement was not only as a promoter of the Ring's claims to vast sections of the land grant but also as a medical doctor who cared for injured people on both sides who fought over land rights. Finally, at one point, he heard that he was the target of a planned lynching by the opposing group. He and his wife fled Cimarron for Santa Fe. He restarted his medical practice there, became noted as a leader in the city and later was appointed justice of the peace.[178]

In 1881, he joined Staab as owners of the Exchange Hotel. The Longwell-Staab ownership team continued until 1895, one of the longest-running management teams to that point in the hotel's history. It is surmised that Staab took the lead in overseeing this acquisition and its continued management.

Longwell attempted to legitimize his landholdings in the former Maxwell Land Grant. The stress of the legal wrangling over the land caused his health to deteriorate, and he returned east for medical help. He passed away in Philadelphia in February 1895.

16
STILL STANDING

When Western enterprise pierces into the yet uncultivated regions…when the log cabin of the distant settler is seen upon the banks of the shallow Arkansas—when cities rise where now the advancing plough has not yet disturbed the sunflower of the tall green blade—then may we hear and listen with interest to the history of early pioneers, and our grandchildren will yet wonder why their fathers and grandfathers spoke not more fluently about the glorious inheritance…of the West.
—*Matt Field,* On the Santa Fe Trail, *87*

In early 1891, Abraham Staab apparently grew weary of trying to manage the hotel in addition to his other large holdings, so he leased the hotel to a new proprietor, John T. Forsha. Forsha's wife, Belle, then became the de facto day-to-day manager. The *Santa Fe New Mexican* spoke glowingly of the hotel's future under Forsha. "Many are the words of praise that genial gentleman has earned by his obliging and kindly manner. Santa Fe's pioneer landlord, Capt. John T. Forsha, of the Exchange hotel."

The hotel consistently ran an advertisement in the local newspaper for nearly nine years claiming that the Exchange was the "Best located Hotel in the City" and had rooms for rent for as low as $1.50 per day. Forsha continued at the hotel until his untimely death in 1902 at age fifty-six.[179]

When on February 2, 1895, merchant Staab lost his devoted partner, Longwell, he gained a new partner. Shortly before his passing, "Robert H. Longwell and his wife conveyed to Hiram H. Cartwright their undivided one-half interest in The Exchange."[180]

Above: Group of hotel staff and city leaders in front of the door to the Exchange Hotel. Abraham Staab is third from right. *Photograph from the La Fonda Hotel archives.*

Opposite: The Exchange Hotel floorplan. *Photograph from the La Fonda Hotel archives.*

Hiram, one of eight children in an Iowa family of English background, learned the retail trade as a clerk in his father's mercantile store in Des Moines. "In 1878 he left his old home and went to Kansas where he was employed in the same capacity until the spring of 1879." He had a keen sense of adventure and decided to hop on the Santa Fe Railway that year, headed for Santa Fe. He also had the urge to go into business on his own, so "he opened a small book-store, which he carried on for two years, with a fair degree of success."

It wasn't long before his business broadened until it became "the largest business of the kind in the city." His establishment covered nearly an entire block at the corner of San Francisco and Don Gaspar Streets. His store carried a "full and complete stock of groceries, provisions and fruits, and large quantities of hay and grain," and "an annual business that would be a credit to a city five times the size of Santa Fe."

As a successful businessman and fellow in the Scottish Rite Temple, Cartwright became a leader in local investments, including mining and

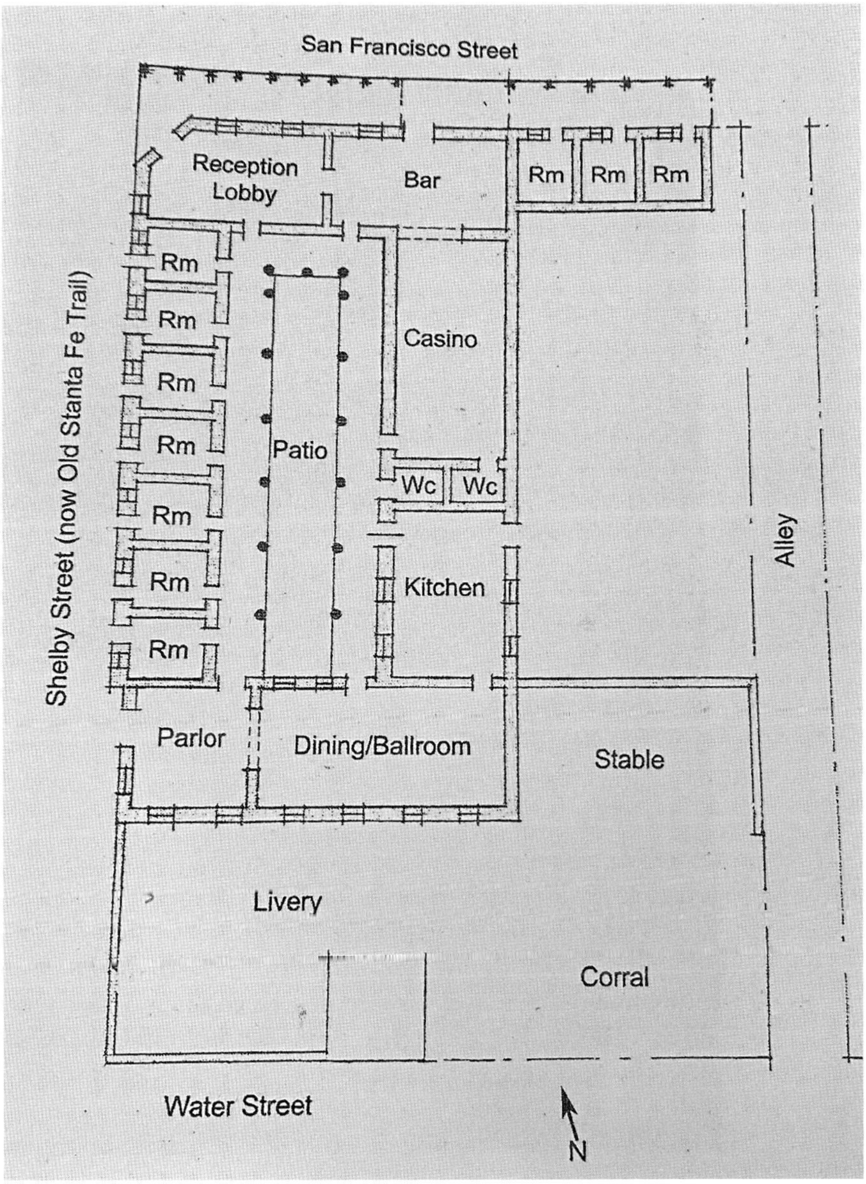
San Francisco Street
Reception Lobby
Bar
Rm
Rm
Rm
Rm
Rm
Rm
Rm
Rm
Rm
Rm
Casino
Patio
Wc
Wc
Kitchen
Shelby Street (now Old Stanta Fe Trail)
Alley
Parlor
Dining/Ballroom
Stable
Livery
Corral
Water Street
N

the Santa Fe Telephone Company. He also served as a director of the new Electric Light Company. He began making real estate investments, one of which was as "half owner of the Exchange Hotel," and he was elected treasurer of Santa Fe County. His brother Samuel came west and joined him in his expanding empire. They named their firm H.B. Cartwright & Brother.

The Staab-Cartwright partnership lasted four years. With Forsha as the hotel proprietor, it seemed to go smoothly. But "on January 2, 1899, H. B. Cartwright conveyed to A. Staab his half interest" in the hotel.[181]

While the old Exchange continued to battle for its existence in Santa Fe, a hotelier by the name of Fred Harvey, in league with the Atchison, Topeka and Santa Fe Railway, was developing a hospitality empire that would eventually command the respect of the nation. Harvey already had restaurants or hotels in Raton and Las Vegas and a small hotel with a restaurant in Lamy, about twenty miles south of Santa Fe. His trackside hotel in Las Vegas was the scene of the national reunion of Teddy Roosevelt's Rough Riders in 1899.

An incident at the Harvey Mountain House restaurant in Raton brought a radical change to personnel policies, probably the first of its kind in America. Many restaurants in the West hired Black waiters and busboys to serve customers, but "many cowboys were former Confederate soldiers who had fled the south because they could not imagine living in peace among freed slaves." A big fight among the Raton waitstaff occurred in 1883, resulting in many injuries. Harvey hurried to the scene, fired the manager and other staff and assigned a new manager, Tom Gable, a family friend.

Gable's solution to the waiters' unrest was to assign Black staff to kitchen duties and import white single women from the Midwest to serve customers at the tables. These young women became known as the "Harvey Girls" of western legend, and many stayed on to found families in the Southwest.[182]

While the Harvey Company was developing its chain restaurant system, most likely the first in America, another ambitious father-son duo was actively welcoming visitors to their small establishment in a little town just south of Albuquerque, San Antonio. Thanks to the installation of railroad tracks leading south along the Rio Grande, Augustus "Gus" H. Hilton and his son Conrad were busy meeting the southbound and northbound trains at the San Antonio station to offer travelers a room for the night. From this humble beginning would grow the first worldwide chain of luxury hotels.

Young Conrad, sometimes called "Connie," learned a great deal from his father about the care of customers and how to make a profit. But by all accounts his father was quite overbearing, and Connie winced under his discipline. "In military school, Connie learned that 'all a man has got is his word. If you can't trust what he says, how do you know he's there at all?' In later years, Connie would frustrate his lawyers and his publicity folks by refusing to bend the truth in the slightest."

With his father's financial backing, he opened a bank in San Antonio, but it was not successful. After failure of the bank, Connie started thinking that he could be much more successful in a larger city. He ended up traveling to Cisco, Texas, where he planned to start a bank, using his own $5,000 personal fund. Cisco was a thriving town in the oil belt, and Connie liked the bustling atmosphere. However, after agreeing on a price, the bank owner upped the price at the last minute. This was definitely not appreciated by Hilton, so he sought a hotel for the night, the run-down Mobley, to think over his situation.

"The lobby was mobbed….Come back in eight hours, when we swap out the rooms," the front desk attendant suggested. Instantly, Connie knew he was vying for the wrong business. The money, he realized, was in the hotel business. His offer to buy the Mobley was accepted, and he soon found himself owner of a hotel. He then proceeded to buy the old Melba Hotel in Fort Worth, then the 150-room Waldorf in Dallas. It was the start of his hotel brand that, in the end, stretched around the world.[183]

As Harvey and Hilton were expanding their empires, back in Santa Fe, the Exchange was about to get a new owner. On September 16, 1907, Abraham Staab sold the building to Thomas Z. Winter, a local grocer. When he purchased it, Winter said, "I have not fully decided just what I will have done to the old building." By this time, use of the building as a hotel was not contemplated because of its crumbling infrastructure, but its location was ideal for other ventures. Winter bought it with plans to locate his grocery business there and was attempting to locate partners who could add customer-attracting businesses to complement his store.

A sympathetic visitor toured the old building soon after Winter bought it and recorded a nostalgic description of the place. It appeared in the *Epworth Herald*, a publication for youth in the Methodist Episcopal Church and was most likely written by the editor when visiting Santa Fe. The writing seems to best describe the nearly one-hundred-year-old edifice at this stage of its life.

> *Next to the palace in years and interest is the old Exchange Hotel, once a famous hostelry at the end of the Santa Fe Trail. It juts into the corner of the Plaza, but as its visible parts are occupied by market, barber shop, and "rooms to let," many a serious tourist passes it by, little dreaming of its history. Over one door on a side street is a quaintly lettered sign: "Parlor," but this is accepted by the stranger as a part of the present lodging house.*
>
> *The hotel was built around two courts, and none of the rooms have walls less than four feet in thickness. A heavy door on the narrow street admits me into a passageway at the old arcade are a fit preparation for the dilapidation of the inner rooms. Dust and disorder, dirt and decay, have possession here.*

Santa Fe's Fonda

The Exchange Hotel in its last days. *Photograph from the La Fonda Hotel archives.*

A crumbling fireplace with rusty skillet clinging to it—paper clutching the ceiling on one side while its dirty length trails the floor—broken furniture hobnobbing with rank weeds—cobwebs throwing their lace work over heaps of rotten boards, all tell of years of neglect. The "Dining rooms" invites us from the placita. An old table and a few dishes recall the time when this was crowded with hungry men from the caravan that had crossed the desert in hope of gain. Then the room was noisy with laughter; while wild tales, seasoned with oaths, accompanied the feasting.

At the back of the second court are stables and corral, and the usual waste of broken adobe. All is gruesome enough with the bright sun as our ally, but what must it be in the black night! Then one would hear the wing of the bat, the hooting of the owl, the scurrying of rats, and if uneasy spirits ever return to former haunts, here would be their starting place. The Exchange was once the goal, the resting place, the attained, after the weary march of long weeks with its perils from Indians, lost trails, lack of water and disease. What happiness again to eat from a table and sleep on a bed, free from duty as sentinel, with no fear of savage cry or howl of beasts![184]

The Story of the Old Inn at the End of the Trail

It took Winter nearly a year of working with his contacts in the city to finally decide how the old building could best be utilized. By December 1908, he had decided that its best use, in addition to his grocery shop, would be to turn the old hotel into a boardinghouse. He turned its management over to Mrs. N.M. Thornton, who previously was in charge of a sanitarium kitchen in town. "The ancient place once the scene of exciting times when it was used as the Exchange Hotel during the balmy days of the Santa Fe Trail has been converted into a very cozy and modern home."[185]

Her daughter Bessie wrote in later years of her stay in the house. For the two years that she lived there, "It was an eating house only. Served noon and evening meals; no breakfast," she said. It was, indeed, different than in earlier days, when dozens of patrons attended. Bessie said there "was a large dining room. There were 4 tables seating 8 people each."[186]

So far there is no record that the building was ever used extensively for lodging purposes after the Thorntons moved out. The local newspaper, as was its custom, continued to list arrivals of VIPs at local hotels. In 1908, important visitors were listed by name in the Palace, the Claire, the Normandie and the Coronado Hotels, but the Exchange was no longer on the list. Modern amenities such as steam-heated rooms, electric lights and telephones were touted as part of accommodations at these other hotels. One, the Claire, even had a telegraph office.

Nevertheless, city leaders who still appreciated the heritage of the Exchange were beginning to realize that it was becoming an eyesore in the downtown Plaza. It became evident that the old building had to be replaced. "At the same time a new spirit was arising in Santa Fe, an enthusiasm for the city's and the region's past and the distinctiveness of New Mexico's architectural traditions."

As old landmarks like the Exchange were beginning to wear out beyond their use date, this new spirit welled up in those who loved the old town. "This zeal for uncovering and reclaiming Santa Fe's heritage would ultimately determine the city's architectural destiny, and along with that of any successor to the old 'American fonda.'"[187]

17
SANTA FE STYLE

It would be perfectly practicable for the inhabitants to build their houses two or more stories high as far as strong walls are necessary for that purpose and the reason why they are not so built is not, as one would at first imagine, because mud walls are inefficient, but because ground is cheap, and the people prefer half a dozen rooms in a row to as many apartments piled one above another. They think it is easier to go through a doorway than up a pair of stairs which is certainly not a very unreasonable conclusion to arrive at. Besides, although timber is plenty, carpenters are scarce, and a board floor is a luxury for which they entertain not the slightest ambition.
—*Matt Field,* On the Santa Fe Trail, *202*

In 1912 an exhibit known as 'New Old Santa Fe' at the Palace of the Governors presented the results of recent research into the characteristics of the region's architecture, despised in earlier decades by visitors and even by its own archbishop." A new vision for the city was presented by the planning board; the effort was to "stimulate tourism and improve civic life through emphasizing historic preservation and a Santa Fe building style." The city was facing a declining population and needed to find a new way to stimulate the economy. Tourism was the conclusion, and "one way to attract tourists would be to fashion a new image from old materials."[188]

The Fred Harvey Company was a leader in New Mexican tourism, and it may have been on the minds of city leaders to look toward the Harvey family as potential partners in the revitalization of the city with the new emphasis on tourism. Fred Harvey died in 1901, and the company was now under the guidance of his son Ford. The railroad "built a new depot and a large mission-style hotel, The Alvarado, in Albuquerque." Next to the hotel, Ford Harvey organized a private building, the "Indian Building," where Native American artists were employed to demonstrate their skills in front of it. "It was like a world's fair exhibit version of Santa Fe, offering train tourists an opportunity to shop like they once could only on the (Santa Fe) Plaza. It was unbelievably successful."

By 1912, Tom Gable, the one-time manager of the Harvey restaurant in Raton, was now resident in Santa Fe and was urging Harvey and the railroad to open a hotel in town. It is doubtful that Gable had the Exchange in mind for a Harvey location. A fire in 1912 further damaged the old structure, making part of it barely a skeleton.

At first, the idea of a Harvey hotel in town was rejected by the family. But cooperation between city and tribal leaders and the Harvey Company in preparation for the World's Fair in San Diego, California, seemed to have some effect on the parties as far as working together after the fair. It would take several years, however, for a result of the congenial cooperation to be fully realized.[189]

"1915 was the first summer after World War I began in Europe, so international tourists had few alternatives but to visit still-neutral America." As a result, tourists poured into the western United States for the first time, "discovering the Grand Canyon and the recently christened 'City Different.'" Then the continuing war and a worldwide flu epidemic stalled tourism for several years, but a rebound occurred in a couple of years.[190]

During this time, however, the idea of a unique architecture for Santa Fe was growing, a "New Mexico Mission Style" as envisioned at the "New Old Santa Fe" exhibit in 1912. "New Mexico's own native and colonial architecture would be restored, preserved, reproduced, and creatively used in a selective version of Santa Fe's past." The concept would soon be heralded in the birth of a new fonda. But not before the old fonda's "ignominious end."[191]

The old Exchange now became a total embarrassment for the city. In the spring of 1916, the city council asked its owner, still T.Z. Winter, to remove the building or face condemnation proceedings. In June, the city once again ordered Winter to remove the building within thirty days or face condemnation. But it would take another three years before something was actually done about the crumbling edifice; nevertheless, its death was near.

The World War II army tank "Mud Puppy" demolishing the old Exchange Hotel in 1919. *Photograph from the La Fonda Hotel archives.*

At war's end, Victory Rallies across the United States took place. It was April 1919, and a Victory Bond Rally was organized in Santa Fe. All the shops were closed, and residents gathered in the Plaza to listen to speeches by World War I heroes and city leaders. But the event that brought the biggest excitement was a scheme for bringing down the old Exchange Hotel.

A tank that had fought in the Argonne was used to smash the walls of the old adobe building. For every $100 war bond that was purchased, the drivers of the tank would attack the remaining walls, sending up dust and door and window frames with it. It could be said that the Exchange was "a casualty of World War I, for it died as a result of injuries from a two-man tank nicknamed the Mud Puppy."[192]

Ironically as the old Exchange was being destroyed, Conrad Hilton was opening his first hotel in Cisco, Texas. While he had no involvement in the new or old fonda, he would one day stand in its public rooms for his wedding.

The building rubble was carried away, and nothing was left of the old hotel but the vacant lot where it stood. While the building ended up a worthless pile of rubble, the empty lot it had occupied for so many years was one of the most valuable pieces of real estate in the city. Exactly a year after the building was demolished, local citizens, mainly business leaders, formed a corporation to undertake a new plan for the property. They called it the Santa Fe Building Corporation. They "issued 4,000 shares of stock, $50 par value each, which were sold to citizens of Santa Fe to finance the construction" of a new hotel.

"Before the end of 1919, the president of the First National Bank announced the successful completion of a subscription drive to raise $200,000 for the building of the new hotel." The architecture firm Rapp, Rapp, and Henrickson was commissioned to prepare a design for the new building.[193]

Isaac Rapp, main partner in the company, was born in Carbondale, Illinois. He learned his trade from his architect father. In 1889, he moved west to Trinidad, Colorado, where he formed a firm with a partner, C.W. Bulger. When that firm dissolved a few years later, he joined his brother William Rapp, and they created the firm Rapp and Rapp. They soon took on a principal partner, Arthur Hendrickson, and became active designing buildings in southern Colorado and in New Mexico.

By the time the firm was commissioned to design the new La Fonda Hotel, their work on strikingly attractive buildings in Roswell at the New Mexico Military Institute, built in 1891, and the New Mexico Territorial Capitol in 1900, were witness to their talent at creating pleasing architecture that comfortably suited the Southwest landscape. Numerous other buildings of their design in southern Colorado also gained public attention as exemplary structures. "But the firm had attracted attention from the planners of the 'New Old Santa Fe' exhibit with, of all things, a warehouse. It was designed for the Colorado Supply Company and stood…in clear view from the train as it ascended Raton Pass."[194]

The warehouse was designed after a mission church at Acoma Pueblo west of Albuquerque. "Rapp's last major commission was the design of the new hotel.…He planned the building around an interior courtyard, like the old Exchange." It featured terraced roofs, balconies and *vigas* projecting out from the walls. But unlike the old building made of adobe bricks, the new walls were made of fired tile blocks made by prisoners at the state penitentiary and reinforced concrete.

Isaac Rapp, credited with establishing the "Santa Fe Style," with his plan for the new La Fonda Hotel. *Photograph from La Fonda Hotel Archives.*

Nevertheless, various historians saw the hotel as the birth of the "Santa Fe Style," and Rapp is seen as its creator.[195]

The new La Fonda began to rise on the southeast corner of the Plaza. The construction was constantly watched by residents and visitors and was finally completed in December 1922, just in time for a Christmas opening. Once again, America's hospitality corner was alive.[196]

18

A HOTEL FOR THE MAKING

To the contemplative traveler an evening scene in this place presents every material to excite interest and pleasure. The town itself, to the eye of an American, is as novel a spectacle as could be found upon the face of old mother earth, and to this novelty is added that peculiar charm pertaining always to evening, but in this place seeming to strike the senses and awaken admiration with greater force.
—*Matt Field,* On the Santa Fe Trail, *235*

The new hotel became a showcase of the Santa Fe style and would remain so for more than one hundred years, but its success was not immediate. "Forty-six rooms were not enough to ensure its success. The new hotel, the pride of Santa Fe but plagued with financial difficulties, closed after only two years."[197]

Meanwhile, the Harvey Company was busy booking its little hotel in Lamy and arranging side trips to Santa Fe until 1923, when a fire burned down the De Vargas Hotel in downtown Santa Fe, where members of the Harvey family and their friends often stayed.[198]

"Then in 1925, with the post-war economy booming and international interest in Santa Fe tourism rising, Ford Harvey was finally convinced to make a move to Santa Fe." A key facilitator in this idea was Hunter Clarkson, head of the company's transportation services at the Grand Canyon branch of the Harvey Company operating around the El Tovar Hotel, the company's main property at that site. He convinced Ford that the company could expand and lead in the tourism industry from the Grand Canyon and across New

The La Fonda Hotel, 1926, with Indian Detours vehicles at front. *Photograph from the La Fonda Hotel archives.*

Mexico by offering sightseeing trips out of Santa Fe. The operation became known as "Detours," with transportation provided in "Harveycoaches."

"So, in 1925, Ford sent his son Freddy to Santa Fe to shop for hotels." The young man had served as a World War I pilot, and his father hoped this assignment would get him more involved in company business. Freddy discovered the new La Fonda: it was one of the "largest buildings constructed since the new vernacular architectural rules were put into place, and it employed the Pueblo Revival style, boasting thick walls and wooden vegas, the logs that vaulted all the ceilings." Freddy found it to be the ideal property for the Harvey Company.[199]

It was soon announced in the *Santa Fe New Mexican* that the Santa Fe Land Improvement Company (SFLIC), a subsidiary of the Santa Fe Railway, would purchase the La Fonda. The SFLIC was organized shortly after the turn of the century in California to establish a forest of eucalyptus trees near San Diego that would supply railroad ties as the tracks were laid in that state. But the eucalyptus wood was found to be too soft for that purpose, so the company changed plans and turned its efforts into developing a new town, Rancho Santa Fe, at that site. As a legally organized company, it was the logical entity to own the new hotel in Santa Fe, New Mexico.[200]

"On May 1, 1926, La Fonda Building Corporation conveyed to the Santa Fe Land Improvement Company, for the sum of $165,000, the land and the new hotel." For those people in Santa Fe who had purchased stock in the La Fonda Building Corporation, all were to be reimbursed, "at a price which will enable them to comply with the trust agreement." The hotel was then leased to the Fred Harvey system.[201]

"The Santa Fe Railway had already established in the public mind a corporate image that suggested a strong connection with Native American culture." Most people arrived in Santa Fe by rail, and the train experience was novel enough, but "they longed for an escape from the train, a chance to venture into the distant mountains and mesas only glimpsed through its windows." The Harvey plan to provide opportunity for Indian Detours out from Santa Fe became an instant success.

The Detours started the same month the hotel was purchased. They were "initially conducted between the Castañeda Hotel in Las Vegas and the Alvarado Hotel in Albuquerque, with an overnight stay at La Fonda and touring of pueblos between the three towns."

Travelers "climbed into luxurious big Packards and Cadillacs bearing Thunderbird logos. These 'Harveycars' were driven by men wearing riding breeches that seemed more appropriate attire for a fox hunt than an exploration of cowboy country.'" Participants were surprised how well the drivers were able to handle sometimes challenging desert situations such as climbing steep hills and approaching the mesas and the desert sands.

Young women guides, called "couriers," accompanied each tour. They were trained by the company and became expert tour guides. "When Detourists returned to La Fonda for the night they could visit the room known as the lecture lounge." In the lounge were large maps, slideshows and lectures to help people understand "what they were seeing."

"The Indian Detours corralled some of the untamed aspects of New Mexico and turned them into the likes of trail horses for dudes." The tours spotlighted Santa Fe as an international destination, but the "La Fonda was losing $500 a night having to refer guests to other hotels for lack of rooms." It became evident that the hotel had to expand to cater to the demand, and those changes were soon to come.[202]

By late 1928, the Harvey Company was operating "twenty-five hotels, forty sit-down restaurants, fifty-four lunchrooms, and the newsstands and gift shops in eighty cities along the Santa Fe. He was also running all the restaurants, soda fountains, and retail stores in union stations in Chicago, Kansas City, St. Louis, Houston, Wichita, Galveston and Fort Worth, as well

The La Fonda Hotel in the 1970s. *Photograph from the La Fonda Hotel Archives.*

as luxury hotel operations at the Grand Canyon and in Santa Fe. He was serving over twelve million meals a year."[203]

A hotel is a second home to everyone who travels. It is a sacred place of repose to the tired traveler, a respite from the eyestrain of the road, a landing place for the backaches of the luggage-toting traveler. In the days of the Exchange, it was even more. Saddle sore, buckboard sore or stagecoach-bruised travelers found the old hotel a luxury in the high desert. Here was delectable food on a table, a roof over one's head and the hominess of all-round exceptional hospitality. Whether you had suffered the horrors of capture, the tiredness of living in the rough or the antics of an overbearing stagecoach driver, you knew there was relief at the end of the trail. A final arrival at the Exchange made you feel like you were at a place akin to heaven.

The La Fonda Hotel took over that role from the old Exchange, but in an even more exuberant way, to satisfy a more modern and inquisitive traveler. True, modes of transportation changed, but the roads were still long and the strain still present. It's always comforting to know there is relief at the end of the day. May the wonderful spirit of service and hospitality always remain to welcome visitors at the Inn at the End of the Trail.

NOTES

Chapter 1

1. The best description of Becknell the person is found in "The Life of William Becknell," by Allan Wheeler in his research on the Old Santa Fe Trail at the home site of The History of the Santa Fe Trail and Its Founder, William Becknell, www.williambecknell.com.
2. His total debt at this time was thought to have been about $1,000, something in the neighborhood of $26,000 in the early twenty-first century, according to an online inflation calculator.
3. Pike's account is well documented in *The Southwestern Journals of Zebulon Pike, 1806–7*, Part 5, "Diary of a Tour made through the Interior Provinces of New Spain."
4. Reports of Mexico's expected independence appeared in the *Missouri Intelligencer* on August 21, 1821, 3, "A Letter from Havana"; October 30, 1821, 3, "The Vice Roy of Mexico"; and November 6, 1821, 2, "From the Items of News."
5. A detailed description of the expedition's stay in Franklin is recorded in James's *Early Western Travels*, 149–55.
6. For an understanding of the financial situation at this time, see a good overview written in 2015, in its historical perspective, by Van Atta, *Wolf by the Ears*.
7. The candidates, including Becknell, were listed in the *Missouri Intelligencer*, July 29, 1820, 2.
8. The results of the election are found in the *Missouri Intelligencer*, September 9, 1820, 3.

9. This information from a newspaper ad by W. Becknell on August 14, 1821, in the *Missouri Intelligencer*, 3, and confirmed by Becknell's journal published in the same newspaper two years later.
10. Becknell is listed as having paid for a ferry license in 1818, as indicated in the Howard County sheriff's notice of money received from June to December 1818, *Missouri Gazette and Public Advertiser*, December 4, 1818, 3. However, it is not clear if he actually managed the ferry or merely used it occasionally for transporting cargo across the river, this being the most convenient place to cross the Missouri in the vicinity.
11. A speech by U.S. congressman John Floyd, as reported in the *Missouri Intelligencer* on February 18, 1823, 3, relates his personal contact with Becknell and the information that only packhorses, not wagons, were used on Becknell's first trip to Santa Fe. On his second trip, in 1822, he did use wagons, according to this report and according to Becknell's own journal.
12. Some students of history have assumed the party crossed on the eventual main route of the Trail at Raton Pass, however, Becknell's description of the pass does not seem to be the pass at Raton as described by many traders who later traversed that route. Most likely, it was at Emory Gap. See Larry Mahon Beachum, "To the Westward: William Becknell and the Beginning of the Santa Fe Trade," *Journal of the West* 28 (April 1989): 6–12. This is part of a special issue entitled "The Mexican Road: Trade, Travel, and Confrontation on the Santa Fe Trail."
13. Details of Becknell's travel to this point come almost exclusively from his journal as published in the *Missouri Intelligencer*, April 22, 1823, 2–3, "Journal of Two Expeditions from Boon's Lick to Santa Fe." Once he met the Spanish dragoons, however, we also have the record of their troop leader, Captain Pedro Ignacio Gallego, in his *Diary of Pedro Ignacio Gallego*, recorded in the days of early November 1821. The diary can be found in the Mexican Archives of New Mexico (MANM), Twitchell Collection, nos. 3 and 120, New Mexico State Records Center and Archives (NMSRCA), Santa Fe, New Mexico.
14. The location and details of the encounter at Puertocito, thought to be about two miles south of today's Las Vegas, New Mexico, is recorded in Captain Gallego's diary referred to in the previous note.

Chapter 2

15. Final developments in Mexico's independence were detailed in Becknell's hometown newspaper, the *Missouri Intelligencer*, on November 6, 1821, 2.

16. The later years of Becknell's life are summarized from an obituary in the *Clarksville Standard* and in *The Handbook of Texas*, online edition by the Texas Historical Association.
17. Thomas James's expedition is documented in great detail in his book *Three Years among the Indians and Mexicans*, printed in 1846. The section with the background quoted here is found in chapter 3, 74–77.
18. Ibid. Details of his trip continue through the end of chapter 3 and into chapter 4.
19. It is significant that he acquired a translator and a house at the same time, in the same paragraph of his reference to Ortise. Mr. Ortise's name was obviously misspelled. The Spanish version would be spelled "Ortiz." The Spanish archives mention a major landowner in Santa Fe by that name who actually held the office of *alcalde*, for which "mayor" would be the equivalent in English. As we shall see, he was positioned to become a landlord in the hospitality business when the Santa Fe Trail opened. Josiah Webb in his *Adventures in the Santa Fe Trade* said, "The Pinos and Ortizes were considered the *ricos*, and those most respected as leaders in society and political influence" (91).
20. The *Gaceta Imperial* was dated November 17, 1821, and had by Christmas been received in the New Mexican capital. A copy can be found in the New Mexico Records Center and Archives. It contains specific instructions for the organizing steps to be taken for establishing a governing body for the newly independent country. With this in hand, government officials had a firm confirmation that independence was now a reality.
21. Many historians have described the city in its different phases, but probably the most authoritative and descriptive narrative about this epoch is by renowned historian Ralph Emerson Twitchell in his 1925 book *Old Santa Fe*.
22. Twitchell says the Santa Fe jail was located next to a chapel, presumably so prisoners could receive the sacraments of the church (Twitchell, *Old Santa Fe*, 156). Some years later, by the time Americans began arriving over the Santa Fe Trail, a jail was installed at one end of the Palace of the Governors (Taylor, *Short Ravelings from a Long Yarn*, 146; Brayer, *Land of Enchantment*, 46).
23. Don Francisco Ortiz is listed numerous times in the Spanish Archives of New Mexico, usually as alcalde (mayor), between 1814 and 1845. His name appears most often as a witness to various land transactions, apparently because he was close at hand as chief magistrate of Santa Fe with this duty as part of his portfolio. See the Spanish Archives of New Mexico, Vol. 1, items 27, 383, 614, 707, 919, 1063 and others in this volume. Several of the items have to do with his own personal land transactions.

24. A historical map, Urrutia's map of 1766, shows row houses from the Old Santa Fe Trail along to the church at the east end of San Francisco Street (New Mexico State Records Center and Archives). According to archival records, a house on the Trail at Rio Chiquita, now Water Street, was owned by Don Francisco Ortiz and Don Higinio Muños (Spanish Archives of New Mexico, Twitchell, vol. 1, no. 1314, of the New Mexico State Records Center and Archives, and apparently was known as *Los Estados Unidos* (United States House) in later years. Twitchell also identifies the owner of the house at the corner of San Francisco Street and the Old Santa Fe Trail: a member of the Pino family, full name not given, in *The Leading Facts of New Mexico History* 2, 138).

Chapter 3

25. See the Spanish Archives of New Mexico, Twitchell, vol. 1, 1314. Twenty-five years later, another trader, Samuel Magoffin, rented one of these houses in 1846. See Susan Magoffin's *Down the Santa Fe Trail and into Mexico*, 103–04. Also Twitchell, *Old Santa Fe, The Story of New Mexico's Ancient Capital* (Sunstone Press, 2007, with facsimile 281 of the 1925 edition) 237n.481.
26. Becknell's report of his first two trips comes from the *Missouri Intelligencer* of April 22, 1823, 2–3.
27. Several sources report on this new order of organization, of which Twitchell is probably the most detailed (Twitchell, *Old Santa Fe*, 186–92).
28. *Niles Weekly Register*, June 10, 1824. Also Twitchell, *Old Santa Fe*, 212–13.
29. Estimates provided by Gregg in *Commerce of the Prairies*, 130.
30. From Becknell's "Journal of the Expeditions from Boon's Lick to Santa Fe," *Missouri Intelligencer*, April 22, 1823, 2–3.
31. Gregg's descriptions of New Mexico's towns at that time come from his notes and newspaper articles that have since been printed in a book of 1844 titled *Commerce of the Prairies*, 36–37.
32. Field's descriptions of Santa Fe and its residents is an enjoyable read, as they are written in poetry and prose in *On the Santa Fe Trail*, 202–18. Most of the book is a compilation of his articles written for the *New Orleans Picayune*.
33. While documentation seems to be lacking about how an inn was created out of the existing houses on the site in question, it should be noted that hotels exist in Santa Fe even today that are made up of groups of houses that were joined together and turned into hotels.
34. Marmaduke kept a diary of the trip, and Chittenden in his *The American Fur Trade of the Far West* gave a detailed account of this enterprise and

said he gained his information from the *Missouri Intelligencer*. Twitchell also gives extensive details in *Old Santa Fe*, 215. The first printed term using the name "Santa Fe Trail" was in the *Missouri Intelligencer* and *Boon's Lick Advertiser*, June 18, 1825, 4.
35. Field, *On the Santa Fe Trail*, 218–20.

Chapter 4

36. Carson, *Kit Carson's Autobiography*, 4.
37. Information obtained from excellent research done by Meyer, *Mary Donoho*, 7–25.
38. Lieutenant Cooke gives an excellent description of the trip in his book *Scenes and Adventures in the Army*, 45–55.
39. From the book by Young, *First Military Escort on the Santa Fe Trail*, 1829; from the *Journal and Reports of Major Bennet Riley and Lieutenant Philip St. George Cooke*, 71–151.
40. Two owners are associated with the houses; Don Francisco Ortiz and Don Higinio Muñoz, as recorded in the Archives of New Mexico, Twitchell, vol. 1, no. 1314, NMSRCA.
41. The story of the Texas incident from the book by Brown, *Indian Wars and Pioneers of Texas*, and from *A Narrative of the Captivity of Mrs. Horn, and Her Two Children, with That of Mrs. Harris, by the Comanche Indians*, by E. House.
42. John Henry Brown, famous early historian of Texas (1820–95), identified Coffee as the founder of Coffee's Trading House on the Red River, who became a member of the Texas congress in 1838. Hunter, *Frontier Magazine*, "Horrors of Indian Captivity to Be Retold," 12.

Chapter 5

43. Information that Mrs. Harris found Mary Donoho in Santa Fe is documented by Brown, *Horrors of Indian Captivity*, last chapter.
44. An excellent summary of the Parkers' story is found in a news article: "Quanah Parker Dead; Famous Comanche Chief Once Entertained Ambassador Bryce," *New York Times*, February 24, 1911, 9.
45. Numbers of men in the trader teams during this period are taken from Gregg, *Commerce of the Prairies*, 130. The same source indicates an average of one hundred wagons per year crossed over the Old Santa Fe Trail from Missouri to Santa Fe during the period.
46. Josiah Gregg, who was in Santa Fe at this time, gives a good description of the dismal education situation, noting that female education was even

more neglected than that of males (*Commerce of the Prairies*, 52). Vivid descriptions of the schools themselves are found in chapter 13.
47. Davis, *El Gringo, New Mexico and Her People*, 186.
48. Twitchell provides extensive detail and background of the insurrection in chapter 7 of *Old Santa Fe*, 197–201. Gregg tells a more man-on-the-street account of what he witnessed in *Commerce of the Prairies*, 130.
49. Lecompte recorded these quotes in *Rebellion in Rio Arriba*, 33–34.
50. Brown, *Horrors of Indian Captivity*, part 3.

Chapter 6

51. Twitchell, *Old Santa Fe*, 201.
52. This information about Armijo's background supplied by Kendall, *Narrative of the Texan Santa Fé Expedition*, 346–47. Journalist Kendall, part of the expedition from Texas in 1841, had ample opportunity to observe and research the governor when the Texas group was taken captive by the Mexicans.
53. Meyer, in *Mary Donoho*, gives an excellent summary of the Donohos' later years in Clarksville (chapters 8 and 9).
54. Field, *On the Santa Fe Trail*, 204.
55. Ibid., 205, 209. Field gives a very detailed description of how the game of monte was played in the section of his book *The Monte Bank*, 209–13.
56. Ibid., 238, 240.
57. Details of the expedition are gleaned from Field, *Route to Santa Fe* (chapter 11), Twitchell, *Texas Santa Fe Expedition* (chapter 7) and Horgan, *Santa Fe Pioneers* (chapter 16).

Chapter 7

58. Details of the political changes at this time are from Twitchell, *Texas Santa Fe Expedition*, 245–49 and Bloom, *Old Santa Fe*, 351–52.
59. Twitchell, *Texas Santa Fe Expedition*, 253.
60. Magoffin, *Down the Santa Fe Trail*, 140.
61. Ibid., 103, 104.
62. Twitchell, *Texas Santa Fe Expedition*, 237. His conclusion was probably based on the description of the center of town by James Josiah Webb, a tradesman at the time who left vivid descriptions of the streets around the Plaza at the time. Webb's book on the subject was printed posthumously.
63. Gregg, *Commerce of the Prairies*, 54.

64. Ruxton's book *Adventures in Mexico and the Rocky Mountains* not only is an excellent story of his visit but also a worthwhile evaluation of the surrounding Native American tribes. He also associates local topography with the movements of the native tribes through history (chapter 33, 189–99).
65. Carson gives the most reliable account of the battle in his autobiography, 109–19.
66. Richard C. Walske, *Mails of the Westward Expansion, 1803 to 1861*, chapter 10.
67. The first Spanish-language newspaper in the city was *El Crepusculo de la Libertad*, which appeared on November 29, 1835, but it only printed four issues according to "First NM Imprint" in the *Princeton University Chronicle* 33, no. 1 (1971): 30–40.
68. From the *Santa Fe Republican*. Davis also gives a good description in *El Gringo*, 166. He also takes his reader on a tour of the city's downtown in chapter 7.
69. Hertzog wrote a very informative essay on the hotel in his *La Fonda*, published in the *Press of the Territorian* in 1964, 6.

Chapter 8

70. The ball in honor of Price was first announced in the *Santa Fe Republican*, 2. It was later reported again in the same newspaper and quoted by Hertzog, *La Fonda*, 4.
71. Horgan, *Lamy of Santa Fe*, 123.
72. Hertzog mentions Tules in his reconstruction of the scene as told by Colonel Francisco Perea, reminiscing in his old age about the event. Other sources mention that the hostess was an American, and if this is true, the designation would eliminate Tules from the role (Hertzog, *La Fonda*, 6).
73. The gruesome story of Governor Bent's murder is graphically told in Cutts, *Conquest of California and New Mexico*, chapter 10, 216–22. The account of these incidents includes a lengthy verbatim report of Colonel Price to his superiors. The Britisher, Ruxton, happened to be in Taos at the time on his trip north and gave another description of the happenings in his book *Old Santa Fe*, 227–29.
74. Duffus, *Santa Fe Trail*, 222.
75. *Santa Fe Republican*, August 8, 1849, 1. The newspaper was having difficulty maintaining its publishing schedule, mainly because of lack of newsprint. This issue of the organ apparently was the last. A new publication, the *Santa Fe New Mexican*, soon became the main source of information.
76. Santa Fe County Records, Deed Records Book A, 153–54.

77. Twain, *Roughing It*, 7. His experience came as a passenger in 1861.
78. Hickok was about twenty years old when he took the job of stage driver with the Overland Stage Company. His biography, *Wild Bill Hickok*, by Frank J. Wilstach, was written in 1926. These quotes about his arrival by stage into Santa Fe appear on page 37.
79. Davis, *El Gringo*, 234.
80. Details of the Exchange Hotel saga during its early years were gathered in a little booklet published in 1964 in Santa Fe by Peter Herzog. The *Press of the Territorian* published a series of booklets about various aspects of territorial history. The account of Bennet's actions and hanging appear in *La Fonda, The Inn of Santa Fe*, 8. In his account, Hertzog intimates that there was a fonda at the site ever since 1609. However, no records have been found to validate that claim.
81. A full, detailed account of Lamy's trip is found in Horgan, *Lamy of Santa Fe*, chapter 4, "The Wreck at Indianola," 94–98.
82. Ibid. The biography of Bishop Lamy by Paul Horgan is excellent, 108, 109.

Chapter 9

83. The descriptions here of the two men are composites of facts found in Johnson, *Last Camel Charge*, 197, and Cheney, "Story of an Emigrant Train," in *The Annals of Iowa*, 84.
84. Biographical note to Leonard John Rose Papers at the Huntington Library, San Marino, California.
85. Johnson, *Last Camel Charge*, 197.
86. The reader is reminded that this was five years before the Arizona Territory was created. At this time, 1858, New Mexico Territory extended to the Colorado River, and that river served as the border between New Mexico and California.
87. Johnson, *Last Camel Charge*, 198.
88. Baley, *Disaster at the Colorado*, 22–23.
89. Johnson, *Last Camel Charge*, 200.
90. President James Buchanan, "Proclamation on the Rebellion in Utah," April 6, 1858.
91. Johnson, *Last Camel Charge*, 203.
92. Cheney, "Story of an Emigrant Train," 4.
93. Johnson, *Last Camel Charge*, 209.
94. Ibid., 221.
95. Ibid., 227.

Chapter 10

96. Jerry Thompson, in the introduction to his book *Confederate General of the West*, gives a colorful and detailed description of Sibley based on his research into the man's life. With little personal information or artifacts to depend on, Thompson came to his conclusions about Sibley with historical accuracy about his known actions. Heavy drinking was Sibley's downfall, as seen in a near court-martial in Mexico, a feud with his superior in Kansas, a court-martial in Utah, controversy during the Navajo Campaign of 1860 and another court-martial in Louisiana and his expulsion as a military advisor in Egypt.
97. Thompson, *Confederate General of the West*, chapter 1, 3–32.
98. Ibid., 32–47.
99. Ibid., 32.
100. United States Patent Office, Patent 14740. The patent application shows his invention from every angle and reveals a simple design that was easy to make and repair in an army workshop, if needed, and easy to manufacture in a factory assembly line. It was called a "simple" invention.
101. An article in the *Amarillo Globe-News* on July 11, 2011, by columnist Delbert Trew gives a detailed account of Sibley's inventions and provides a pathetic but comical twist to the story when Sibley decides to resign his position and join the army of the Confederate States of America, 4.
102. Description card in the collection of artifacts at the Hagley Museum and Library, Wilmington, Delaware, where the projectile is on display.
103. Thompson, *Confederate General of the West*, 209.
104. Ibid., chapter 8, 24–56.
105. Ibid., 216.
106. Twitchell, *Old Santa Fe*, 375–79.
107. Thompson, *Confederate General of the West*, 277.
108. *Santa Fe Gazette*, note 43
109. Thompson, *Confederate General of the West*, 292.
110. Twitchell, *Old Santa Fe*, note, 237. While biographer Thompson says Sibley stayed in Albuquerque during most of the battles taking place at Glorieta between his army and the Union army, Twitchell and a couple other historians living closer to the time claim the general stayed at the Exchange during that entire time. Thompson agrees that Sibley traveled to Santa Fe at the end of the battles, so a logical conclusion is that he stayed at both locations for different amounts of time.
111. Horgan, *Lamy of Santa Fe*, 292.
112. *Santa Fe Gazette*, n50.

113. New Mexico State Records Center & Archives, Criminal Court Cases, Territory of New Mexico, Charles G. Parker, Santa Fe County District Court, Criminal Cases, August 1862.
114. *Weekly New Mexican*, July 29, 1864, 2.
115. Thompson, *Confederate General of the West*, 307.
116. Ibid., 344.
117. Ibid., 356.
118. Ibid., 361–68.

Chapter 11

119. Twitchell, *Old Santa Fe*, 386–87.
120. *Weekly New Mexican*, August 8, 2.
121. Twitchell, *Old Santa Fe*, 238n.
122. Ibid., 239, note.
123. *Weekly New Mexican*, July 29, 1864, 2.
124. *Santa Fe Gazette*, September 23, 1871, 2, and May 15, 1872, 2.
125. Horgan, *Lamay of Santa Fe*, 299.
126. Sides, *Blood and Thunder*, 412.
127. Ibid., 413 and 416.
128. Ibid., 300.
129. Ibid., 407. While Sides does not claim his book to be a biography of Carson, it does serve as a complete essay of the famous man who dominated the news out of New Mexico in the mid- to late 1800s.
130. Jay W. Sharp, "The Long Walk Trail: The Navajos," Desert USA, https://www.desertusa.com.
131. Ibid.
132. Twitchell, *Old Santa Fe*, 292–93.

Chapter 12

133. Darlis A. Miller, "William Logan Rynerson in New Mexico, 1862–1893," *New Mexico Historical Review* 48, no. 2 (2021). Miller gives an extensive treatment of the event in the article, with a perceptive insight into the accounts given by various sources of the day. The author's book *The California Column in New Mexico* gives a robust overview of all members of the column who contributed to New Mexico society.
134. Hertzog, *La Fonda*, 11–13.
135. *Santa Fe New Mexican*, January 14, 1868, 2.

136. *Santa Fe Weekly Gazette*, December 31, 1867, 1.
137. Ibid. Details of the incident in the local newspapers were highly editorialized, and their versions depended on which of the leading political parties they espoused.
138. Miller, "William Logan Rynerson," 105.
139. Ibid., 126.
140. Otero, *Real Billy the Kid*, 7. Numerous books about Billy the Kid exist, and just as many try to prove the real story of Billy, one of the most notable gunmen in the West. The Otero book appears to be one of the more accurate and was written journalistically closer to the events involving the Kid. For various options on the story, see the bibliography.
141. The American History and Genealogy Project, John Martin and Family, Doña Ana County, New Mexico, from *History of New Mexico, Its Resources and People*, by N. Anderson, Volume II.
142. Hertzog, *La Fonda*, 13–14.
143. Ibid., 14.
144. Leckie, *Buffalo Soldiers*, 26.
145. Hertzog, *La Fonda*, 15.
146. Ibid., 16.

Chapter 13

147. Miller, *California Column in New Mexico*, 156. The newspaper advertisement appears in Hertzog, *La Fonda*, 15.
148. Hertzog, *La Fonda*, 21.
149. Boomhower, *Sword & the Pen*, 97. The author was writing his biography of Wallace in the twenty-first century and, like many others, referred to the Exchange Hotel by the name of its replacement, the La Fonda Hotel. The use of the name of the later hotel can confuse readers unless they keep in mind that the Exchange Hotel was demolished in 1919.
150. S. Wallace, *Land of the Pueblos*, 13.
151. Boomhower, *Sword & the Pen*, 98–101.
152. Twitchell, *Old Santa Fe*, 396.
153. Steele, *Santa Fe 1880*, 110.
154. Ibid., 147.
155. *Weekly Santa Fe New Mexican*, February 14, 1880, 3.
156. Hertzog, *La Fonda*, 22–23.

Chapter 14

157. Niederman, *Quilt of Words*, 25. The author reprinted a story originally written by Flora Spiegleberg many years previous in *American Hebrew Journal*, 1820.
158. Ibid, Steele, 74–75.
159. Ibid., 76.
160. Ibid., 90.
161. *Santa Fe New Mexican*, August 23, 1880, 2. Twitchell confirms the fact in *Old Santa Fe*.
162. *American Hebrew Journal*, November 2, 1920, 858.
163. Steele, *Santa Fe 1880*, 121.
164. *Santa Fe New Mexican*, December 29, 1880, 1.
165. Ibid., May 3, 1880, 1. The notice, in the form of an advertisement, appeared numerous times beginning on this date and apparently continued appearing up to early December. Garret, as the one apprehending Billy, waited some months to obtain his reward until the territorial legislature finally voted to award it. But in the end, Garret received several thousand dollars as reward from New Mexican citizens who were pleased to be rid of the gunslinger of Lincoln County.
166. Ibid., December 30, 1880, 1.
167. *Quivira Society Magazine*, "Letters of Adolph Bandelier," 1949,

Chapter 15

168. Hertzog, *La Fonda*, 21. The purchase of the hotel by Longwell and Staab is also confirmed in landholding research done by Linda Tigges, "Santa Fe Landownership in the 1880s," *New Mexico Review* 68, no. 2, Article 4, 173.
169. "A Legend, Going Strong," *New Mexico Magazine* (January 2012).
170. Hertzog, *La Fonda*, 24.
171. Grave headstone history at Fairview Cemetery in Santa Fe from online Find a Grave.
172. Twitchell, *Old Santa Fe*, 497.
173. Hannah Nordhaus, https://www.hannahnordhaus.com/julia/page/2.
174. Michelsohn, *Billy the Kid in Santa Fe, Book One*, 134.
175. Ibid., 137.
176. Grave headstones at Fairview Cemetery, Santa Fe.
177. Grave headstone history, Evergreen Cemetery, Gettysburg, Pennsylvania, from Find a Grave. Two different spellings of Longwell's name are found in various historical reports at this time; some spelled it "Longwill." In the

family mentions of him, the spellings with *e* are used, and it is assumed that their spelling of the family name would be most accurate.
178. Ibid.

Chapter 16

179. *Santa Fe Daily New Mexican*, August 4, 1894, 1.
180. Hertzog, *La Fonda*, 25. Hertzog's book states that the date Longwell joined the partnership was 1899. This date was obviously a misprint because Longwell died in 1895. An entry in the Biographies of Des Moines County, Iowa, written in 1895, states correctly, that H.B. Cartwright was an owner of the Exchange in the year of its writing, 1895.
181. Hertzog, *La Fonda*, 25.
182. Fried, *Appetite for America*, 86–87.
183. *Handbook of Texas*, "Hilton, Conrad Nicholson (1887–1979)." Biography entry by Diana J. Kleiner, information confirmed by Conrad Hilton's brief biography by the Archbridge Institute, written by Gary Hoover.
184. *Epworth Herald*, December 28, 1907, 9. The *Epworth Herald* was published from 1890 until 1940 as the official newspaper of the Epworth League, a young people's service organization within the Methodist Episcopal Church from 1890 until 1940.
185. Hertzog, *La Fonda*, 26. The action was confirmed by Arthur Scott in a narrative about the hotel in the online Voces de Santa Fe, From Old Fonda to La Fonda, https://brotmanblog.com/tag/nusbaum, April 19, 2015.
186. Hertzog, *La Fonda*, 27.
187. Lynn, *Windows on the Past*, 36.

Chapter 17

188. Ibid, 36.
189. Stephen Fried, "Living History," *Santa Fe Reporter*, August 2, 2013, 5.
190. Ibid.
191. Ibid.; Lynn, *Windows on the Past*, 37.
192. Ibid., 37.
193. Hertzog, *La Fonda*, 28. Some historians, writing of the event, said that whoever bought a $100 bond had the opportunity to drive the Mud Puppy as it attacked the walls. Given logical safety concerns for such an activity, it is doubtful this was the case. A vehicle of this type must have had drivers who knew how to maneuver it. But it is conceivable that bond purchasers

may have been given the option of riding in the tank with the driver as it did its demolition work.
194. Isaac Hamilton Rapp, Find a Grave, Memorial ID: 86519. In New Mexico, Rapp and Rapp designed and built the Chaves County Courthouse in Roswell, the La Fonda Hotel in Santa Fe, the New Mexico Military Institute in Roswell and the Mew Mexico Museum of Art in Santa Fe. In Colorado, Rapp and Rapp designed and built many structures in the Trinidad area that are registered in the National Register of Historic Places, including the Zion's German Lutheran Church, the First Baptist Church, the Nichols House, East Street School, the Huerfano County High School and the First Christian Church.
195. Lynn, *Windows on the Past*, 38. At one time serving as a tour guide at the La Fonda, author Steele was shown the penitentiary block wall. The walls are no longer in public view.
196. The Christmas date is found in research developed in an unnamed timeline document in the hotel archives.

Chapter 18

197. Lynn, *Windows on the Past*, 38.
198. Fried, *La Fonda*, 5.
199. Ibid., 14.
200. Rancho Santa Fe Association History webpage, https://www.rsfassociation.org/Club/Scripts/Home/home.
201. Hertzog, *La Fonda*, 28–29.
202. Lynn, *Windows on the Past*, 38–39.
203. Fried, *Appetite for America*, 301.

BIBLIOGRAPHY

Archival Materials

The Diary of Pedro Ignacio Gallego, Mexican Archives of New Mexico #3 & 120, New Mexico State Records Center and Archives (NMSRCA). Santa Fe, New Mexico.

The Gaceta Imperial Extraordinaria de Mexico, Tom I, No. 30, 217. New Mexico State Records Center and Archives (NMSRCA). Santa Fe, New Mexico.

The Unfinished Autobiography of Henry Hastings Sibley. The Minnesota Historical Collections, J. Fletcher Williams' "Henry Hastings Sibley, a Memoir." Minnesota Historical Collections, 6: 257–310.

United States Patent Office. Patent 14740 Conical Tent, H.H. Sibley, United States Army, April 22, 1856.

———. Patent 225,650,Projectile, H.H. Sibley, United States Army, April 22, 1856.

Newspapers

Amarillo Globe News
Albuquerque Journal
Las Vegas Optic

Missouri Commonwealth
Missouri Gazette and Public Advertiser
Missouri Intelligencer

BIBLIOGRAPHY

National Intelligencer
New Orleans Picayune
New York Times
Niles (MO) Weekly Register
Reveille (Camden County, Missouri)
San Francisco Call
Santa Fe Daily New Mexican
Santa Fe Gazette
Santa Fe Reporter
Santa Fe Republican
Santa Fe Weekly New Mexican
Standard (Clarksville, TX)
Van Buren County (IA) Register

Unpublished Sources

Find a Grave. Abraham Staab. www.findagrave.com.

Genealogy Trails History Group. *Biographies of Des Moines County, Iowa.*

New Mexico State Records Center & Archives. Criminal Court Cases. Territory of New Mexico, Charles G. Parker. Santa Fe County District Court, Criminal Cases, August 1862.

Patent Model. *Projectile Henry Hopkins Sibley*, inventor. March 16, 1880, 2015.14.3142. Hagley Museum and Library. Wilmington, Delaware.

Pearson, Jeffrey V. "Philip St. George Cooke: On the Vanguard of Western Expansion with the U.S. Army, 1827–1848." Dissertation. University of New Mexico, May 2011.

Rose, Leonard John. *Leonard John Rose Papers, 1858–1899.* Huntington Library. San Marino, California.

Santa Fe County Courthouse. Deed Records: Books A & P-1, Santa Fe, New Mexico.

Tiedeman, Terry. *Walk Through Turn of the Century Santa Fe.* Map and Historical Sketch.

Secondary Resources

American Hebrew. Philip Cohen, publisher. *Flora Spiegleberg's Reminiscences.* New York: American Hebrew Publishing Company, 1879.

Anderson, George B., ed. *History of New Mexico, Its Resources and People.* Vol. 1. Los Angeles: Pacific States Publishing Company, 1907.

Baley, Charles W. *Disaster at the Colorado.* Boulder: University Press of Colorado, 2002.

Ball, Larry D. *The United States Marshals of New Mexico and Arizona Territories, 1846–1912.* Albuquerque: New Mexico University Press, 1978.

Bibliography

Barnum, Charles, and Judy White. *The American History and Genealogy Project, Newspapers of New Mexico, 1996 and 2016.* https://nmahgp.genealogyvillage.com/newspapers_of_new_mexico.html.

Binkley, William Campbell. *Southwestern Historical Quarterly* 27, no. 2, *New Mexico and the Texan Santa Fe Expedition.* Austin, TX: October 1923.

Bloom, Lansing B. *Old Santa Fe.* New Mexico Quarterly Review articles.

Boomhower, Ray E. *The Sword & the Pen: A Life of Lew Wallace.* Indianapolis: Indiana Historical Society Press, 2011.

Brayer, Garnet M, ed. *Land of Enchantment.* Evanston, IL, 1954.

Brown, John Henry. *Indian Wars and Pioneers of Texas.* Austin, TX: I.E. Daniel, 1890.

———. *The Horrors of Indian Captivity.* Bandera, TX: J. Marvin Hunter, 1954.

Bryant, Keith L. *History of the Atchison, Topeka and Santa Fe Railway.* Lincoln: University of Nebraska Press, 2011.

Burns, Walter Noble. *The Saga of Billy the Kid, The Thrilling Life of America's Original Outlaw.* New York: Skyhorse Publishing, 1925.

Carson, Kit. *Kit Carson's Autobiography.* Edited by Milo Milton Quaife. Lincoln: University of Nebraska Press, 1966.

Chamberlain, Kathleen P. *Victorio.* Norman: University of Oklahoma Press, 2006.

Chavez, Thomas C. *An Illustrated History of New Mexico.* Chicago: Lewis Publishing Company, 1845.

———. *New Mexico Past and Future.* Albuquerque: University of New Mexico Press, 2006.

Cheney, J.W. "The Story of An Emigrant Train." *Annals of Iowa* 12 (1915).

Chittenden, Hiram Martin. *The American Fur Trade of the Far West.* New York: Press of the Pioneers, 1935.

Cline, Donald. *Alias Billy the Kid: The Man Behind the Legend.* Santa Fe, NM: Sunstone Press, 1986.

Cooke, Philip St. George. *Scenes and Adventures in the Army: or Romance of Military Life.* Philadelphia: Lindsay & Blakston, 1857.

Coues, Elliott, ed. *The Journal of Jacob Fowler.* New York: Francis P. Harper, 1898.

Cutts, James Madison. *The Conquest of California and New Mexico in the Years 1846 & 1847.* Philadelphia: Carey & Hart, 1847.

Davis, William Watts Hart. *El Gringo, New Mexico and Her People.* Lincoln: University of Nebraska Press, 1982.

Duffus, Robert L. *The Santa Fe Trail.* New York: Longmans, Green and Co., 1930.

Bibliography

Edwards, David G. *Billy the Kid as He Was Reported in Newspapers from 1870's and 1880's.* (no publisher cited in this publication.)

Epworth Herald, December 28, 1907.

Farjola, Richard C., and Steven C. Walske. *Mails of the Westward Expansion 1803–1861.* San Francisco, CA: Western Cover Society, 2015.

Fialka, John J. *Sisters: Catholic Nuns and the Making of America.* London: Macmillan, 2004.

Field, Matt. *On the Santa Fe Trail.* Norman: University of Oklahoma Press, 1839.

Fried, Stephen. *Appetite for America: Fred Harvey and the Business of Civilizing the Wild West—One Meal at a Time.* New York: Random House, 2011.

———. *La Fonda, Then and Now.* Santa Fe: La Fonda Holdings, 2016.

Frost, Richard H. *The Railroad and the Pueblo Indians.* Salt Lake City: University of Utah Press, 2016.

Garrett, Pat F. *The Authentic Life of Billy the Kid.* Santa Fe: New Mexico Printing and Publishing Company, 1882.

Greer, James K. *Colonel Jack Hays: Texas Frontier Leader and California Builder.* College Station: Texas A&M University Press, 1987.

Gregg, Josiah A. *Commerce of the Prairies.* New York: Pantianos Classics, 1844.

Hammond, George P., and Edgar F. Goad. *A Scientist on the Trail, Travel Letters of A.F. Bandelier, 1880–1881.* Berkeley: Quivira Society, 1949.

Handbook of Texas. Texas Historical Association. Austin, Texas.

Hertzog, Peter. *La Fonda, the Inn of Santa Fe.* Santa Fe, NM: Press of the Territorian, 1964.

Hoover, Gary. *Conrad Hilton's Brief Biography.* Washington, D.C.: Archbridge Institute, 2019.

Horgan, Paul. *Great River: The Rio Grande in North American History.* Middletown, CT: Wesleyan University Press, 1984.

———. *Lamy of Santa Fe, His Life and Times.* New York: Farrar, Straus and Giroux, 1975.

House, E., ed. *A Narrative of the Captivity of Mrs. Horn, and Her Two Children, with That of Mrs. Harris, by the Comanche Indians.* St. Louis, MO: C. Keemle, 1839.

Hunter, J. Marvin. *Frontier Magazine* 14, no. 5 (February 1937).

Inman, Henry. *The Story of the Old Santa Fe Trail.* New York: Macmillan Company, 1899.

James, Thomas. *Early Western Travels.* Vol. 14. Cleveland, OH: Arthur H. Clark Company, 1905.

———. *Three Years Among the Indians and Mexicans.* Waterloo, IL: Printed at the Office of the War Eagle, 1846.

Bibliography

Johnson, Forrest Bryant. *The Last Camel Charge*. New York: Berkley Caliber, 2012.

Julyan, Robert. *The Place Names of New Mexico*. Albuquerque: University of New Mexico Press, 1998.

Kendall, George Wilkins. *Narrative of the Texan Santa Fé Expedition*. Chicago: Lakeside Classics, 1929.

Kenner, Charles L. *Buffalo Soldiers and Officers of the Ninth Cavalry, 1867–1898*. Norman: University of Oklahoma Press, 1967.

Leckie, William H. *The Buffalo Soldiers*. Norman: University of Oklahoma Press, 1967.

———. *The Buffalo Soldiers: A Narrative of the Negro Cavalry in the West*. Norman: University of Oklahoma Press, 1967.

Lecompte, Janet. *Rebellion in Rio Arriba, 1837*. Albuquerque: University of New Mexico Press, 1985, 17.

Lynn, Sandra. *Windows on the Past: Historic Lodgings of New Mexico*. Albuquerque: University of New Mexico Press, 1999.

Magoffin, Susan Shelby. *Down the Santa Fe Trail and into Mexico*. Lincoln: University of Nebraska Press, 1926, 1962.

Marshall, James. *Santa Fe: The Railroad that Built an Empire*. New York: Random House, 1945.

Meyer, Marian. *Mary Donoho, New First Lady of the Santa Fe Trail*. Santa Fe, NM: Ancient City Press, 1991.

Michelsohn, Lynn. *Billy the Kid in Santa Fe, Book One: Young Billy*. Roswell, NM: Cleanan Press, 2014.

———. *Billy the Kid in Santa Fe, Book Two: A Confining Winter*. Santa Fe, NM: Cleanan Press, 2019.

———. *Billy the Kid's Jail. Santa Fe, New Mexico*. Santa Fe, NM: Cleanan Press, 2011.

Miller, Darlis A. *The California Column in New Mexico*. Albuquerque: University of New Mexico Press, 1982.

Nash, Jay Robert. *Encyclopedia of Western Lawmen & Outlaws*. New York: Paragon House, 1992.

New Mexico Magazine. "A Legend, Going Strong" (Travel section). January 2012.

Niederman, Sharon. *A Quilt of Words, Women's Diaries, Letters & Original Accounts of Life in the Southwest 1860–1960*. Boulder: Johnson Books, 1988.

New Mexico Historical Review 48, no. 2.

Otero, Miguel Antonio Jr. *The Real Billy the Kid*. Houston: Arte Público, 1988. Historical Reprint of the Original Book of 1848.

Pacific States Publishing Co. *History of New Mexico, Its Resources and People*. Vol. I. Los Angeles: Pacific States Publishing.

Pike, Zebulon M. *The Southwestern Expedition of Zebulon M. Pike*. Chicago: Lakeside Press, R.R. Donnelley & Sons, 1925.

Plummer, Rachel. *Rachael Plummer's Narrative of Twenty-one Months Servitude as a Prisoner Among the Comanche Indians*. Edited by William Reese. Austin, TX: Jenkins Publishing Company, 1977.

Prince, L. Bradford. *Spanish Mission Churches of New Mexico*. Cedar Rapids, IA: n.p., 1915.

Princeton University Chronicle. "First NM Imprint," 33, no. 1 (1971).

Rancho Santa Fe Association webpage, History: www.rsfassociation.org/club/scripts/library/view_document.asp?NS=PUBLIC&DN=HISTORY.

Reeves, Frank, ed. "The Charles Bent Papers." *New Mexico Historical Review* 30, no. 21955.

Rittenhouse, Jack D. *Trail of Conquest: A Brief History of the Road to Santa Fe*. Albuquerque: University of New Mexico Press, 1971, 1987 and 2000.

Ruxton, George Frederick Augusta. *Adventures in Mexico and the Rocky Mountains*. London: John Murray, 1847.

Schroeder, Albert, ed. *The Wonderful Year of 1880*. Santa Fe, NM: La Gaceta, El Corral de Santa Fe Westerners 5, no. 3, 1971.

Segale, Sister Blandina. *At the End of the Santa Fe Trail*. Milwaukee, WI: Bruce Publishing Company.

Sides, Hampton. *Blood and Thunder*. New York: Anchor Books, 2006.

Simmons, Marc. *New Mexico, An Interpretive History*. New York: Norton, 1977.

———. *Opening the Santa Fe Trail*. Cerrillos, NM: Galisteo Press, 1971.

———. *Yesterday in Santa Fe*. Santa Fe, NM: Sunstone Press, 1989.

Steele, Allen R. *Santa Fe 1880*. Charleston, SC: The History Press, 2019.

Sunder, John E., ed. *Matt Field on the Santa Fe Trail*. Norman: University of Oklahoma Press, 1960.

Taylor, Benjamin F. *Short Ravelings from a Long Yarn*. Santa Anna, CA: Fine Arts Press, 1936, 146.

Thompson, Jerry. *Confederate General of the West*. Natchitoches, LA: Northwestern State University Press, 1987.

Tigges, Linda. "Santa Fe Landownership in the 1880s." *New Mexico Historical Review* 68, no. 2 (1993).

Twain, Mark. *Roughing It*. A publication of the Mark Twain Project of the Bancroft Library. Berkeley: University of California Press, 1995.

Twitchell, Ralph Emerson. *The Leading Facts of New Mexico History*. Vol. 2. Albuquerque, NM: Horn and Wallace, 1963, 146

———. *Old Santa Fe: The Story of New Mexico's Ancient Capital.* Santa Fe: Santa Fe New Mexican Publishing, 1925.

Van Atta, John R. *Wolf by the Ears, The Missouri Crisis, 1819–1821.* Baltimore, MD: Johns Hopkins University Press, 2015.

Voces de Santa Fe online history, in a narrative by Arthur Scott: *From Old Fonda to La Fonda*, April 19, 2015. http://www.vocesdesantafe.org/explore-our-history/santa-fe/1207-from-old-fonda-to-la-fonda.

Wallace, Lew. *Lew Wallace, An Autobiography.* New York: Harper & Brothers, 1906.

Wallace, Susan E. *The Land of the Pueblos.* New York: Provident Book Company, 1888.

Webb, James Josiah, Ralph P Bieber, ed. *Adventures in the Santa Fe Trade, 1844–1847.* Glendale, CA: Arthur H. Clark Company, 1931.

Weddle, Jerry. *Antrim Is My Stepfather's Name, The Boyhood of Billy the Kid.* Tucson: Arizona Historical Society, Historical Monograph no. 9, 1993.

Wilstach, Frank J. *Wild Bill Hickok: The Prince of Pistoleers.* New York: Garden City Publishing, 1926.

Young, Otis E. *The First Military Escort on the Santa Fe Trail.* Glendale, CA: Arthur H. Clark Company, 1952.

———. *The West of Philip St. George Cooke.* Glendale, CA: Arthur H. Clark Company, 1955.

INDEX

A

Apache tribe 92
Arkansas River 16, 17, 18, 22, 23, 40, 41, 117
Armijo, Manuel 54, 55, 56, 57, 59, 60, 61, 138
Arrow Rock, Missouri 15
Atchison, Topeka and Santa Fe Railway 104
Atkinson-Long Expedition 14
Axtell, Samuel B. 102

B

Baca, Bartolomé, governor 33
Baca, Francisco 70
Baker, John D. 92
Bandelier, Adolph 111
Barboncito, Chief 94
Barceló, Maria Gertrudes 56
Battle of Glorieta Pass 85, 97
Battle of San Pasqual 65
Beale, Edward 65, 77, 78, 79, 92

Beales, John Charles 43
Becknell, William 7, 13, 14, 15, 16, 17, 18, 19, 20, 21, 22, 23, 26, 29, 30, 31, 32, 33, 34, 37, 40, 69, 133, 134, 135, 136
Ben Hur (book) 108
Bent, Charles 40, 41, 64, 68, 139
Bent's Fort 16, 25, 26, 33, 40, 50, 82, 83, 121, 131
Billy the Kid 98, 103, 110, 111, 114, 115, 143, 144
Blake, C. E. 91
Boone, Nathan 13
Bosque Redondo 93
Bowler, Thomas 66
Brown, Alpha 75, 79
Buffalo Soldiers 100

C

Camino Real 30
Carleton, James H. 92, 93, 94, 97, 99
Carson, Kit 40, 65, 84, 85, 90, 92, 94
Cartwright, Hiram H. 117, 118, 119, 120, 145

Index

Chávez, Mercedes 103
Cherokee tribe 23
Chihuahua, Mexico 14, 23, 30, 33, 56, 61, 65, 66, 87
City Different 125
Cody, Buffalo Bill 71
Cordaro (chief) 25, 27, 28

D

Davis, Jefferson 77, 84, 89, 115
Davis, S.B. 65, 71, 77, 84, 89, 101, 106, 112, 138, 139, 140
Detours 131
Donoho, Mary 41, 43, 46, 47, 48, 49, 50, 51, 52, 53, 56, 68, 137, 138
Donoho, William 7, 13, 15, 22, 40, 41, 43, 46, 47, 48, 49, 56, 98, 111, 127, 134, 142

E

Eau Post, Arkansas 23
Exchange Hotel 69, 71, 74, 77, 80, 85, 87, 91, 92, 94, 98, 100, 101, 106, 107, 109, 111, 113, 116, 119, 121, 123, 126, 140, 143

F

Florence, S.C. 70
Forsha, John T. 117, 120
Fort Marcy 65
Fort Osage, Missouri 16
Franklin, Missouri 13, 39

G

Gallego, Pedro Ignacio 19
Garland, D.S. 91
Garret, Pat 110
Gonzales, José 55

Governor Facundo Melgares 27, 33
Grant, Ulysses S. 108
Green, Frank 66
Gregg, Josiah 34, 50, 135, 137, 138

H

Harvey, Ford 130
Harvey, Fred 120, 121, 124, 125, 129, 130, 131
Hickok, Wild Bill 70
Hilton, Conrad 120, 126, 145
Hinckley, C.S. 91
Horn, Sarah Ann 43, 45, 46, 47, 48, 49, 53, 137
Humphrey and Coulter 66

I

Inn at the End of the Trail 41, 65, 69, 132

J

James, Thomas 7, 22, 23, 25, 26, 28, 29, 30, 33, 34, 41, 60, 65, 84, 133, 135, 138, 139, 140

K

Kearney, Stephen Watts 61
Kendall, George Wilkins 58
Kiowa tribe 30

L

Lamar, Mirabeau Bonaparte 57
Lamy, J.B. 103
Lamy, Jean Baptiste 73, 99
Lamy, Mercedes 104
Lewis and Clark 16
Lincoln County War 103
Little Rock, Arkansas 23

INDEX

Longwell, Robert 112
Louisiana Territory 14, 15

M

Magoffin, Samuel 61, 65, 84, 136, 138
Magoffin, Susan 51, 61, 136
Mallet, François 104
Martin, John 98, 99, 100, 101, 143
McDonald, Thomas 92
Melgares, Facundo 20
Mitchell, Robert B. 96
Mojave tribe 78
Mormon Troubles 76
Mormon War 77
Mud Puppy 126

N

Navajo tribe 93, 141

O

Oakley, Annie 71
Ortiz, Don Francisco 7, 27, 29, 31, 32, 36, 70, 135, 136, 137
Ortiz, Francisco 7
Osage tribe 15, 16, 23, 32

P

Palace of the Governors 30, 56, 61, 102, 108, 109, 124, 135
Parker, Charles G. 87, 92, 142
Parker, Cynthia Ann 50
Parker Fort 49
Parker-Plummer, Rachel 49
Parker, Quanah 50
Pecos Pueblo 21
Pecos River 20, 26, 47, 93, 94
Pecos village 20, 21, 26, 30, 47, 93, 94, 111
Pérez, Albino 52

Pike, Zebulon 11, 14, 30, 40, 133
Polk, James K. 60
Price, Sterling W. 67
Prince, L. Bradford 104
Pueblo tribes 12

Q

Quapaw tribe 23

R

Rapp, Isaac 127
Raton Pass, New Mexico 18, 98, 127, 134
Raymond and Wood 69
Republic of Texas 43, 57
Rio Grande 12, 14, 30, 43, 44, 47, 57, 61, 65, 85, 94, 99, 120
Rocky Mountains 12, 26, 40, 57, 64, 74
Rose, Leonard 75, 140
Rubideau, Luis 56
Ruxton, George Frederick Augustus 64
Rynerson, William Logan 97, 98, 142

S

San Francisco Street 12, 29, 31, 32, 36, 46, 48, 52, 61, 63, 74, 92, 99, 103, 106, 111, 112, 136
San Miguel del Vado, New Mexico 20, 21, 26, 30, 47, 59
Santa Ana 45, 57
Santa Fe Building Corporation 127
Santa Fe Pioneers 57, 60
Santa Fe Plaza 12, 96, 104
Santa Fe Ring 102, 116
Santa Fe Trail 7, 12, 16, 22, 31, 32, 36, 37, 41, 51, 61, 63, 69, 70, 87, 94, 99, 100, 106, 107, 111, 114, 121, 123, 134, 135, 136, 137, 138
Segale, Blandina 114

INDEX

Sherman, William T. 94, 109
Sibley, Henry Hopkins 81
Sibley Tent 82
Slough, John P. 97, 98
Spiegelberg, Flora 108, 109
Staab, Abraham 112, 113, 114, 121

T

Taos, New Mexico 21, 29, 30, 40, 48, 55, 56, 65, 68, 83, 94, 139
Taylor, Zachary 61, 82
Thornton, N. M. 123

U

United States House 32, 67
Ute tribe 92

W

Wallace, Lew 102, 103, 104, 107, 108, 110, 111, 143
Wickliffe, William N. 41
Winter, Thomas Z. 121

Y

Yellowstone Expedition 14
Young, Brigham 76, 77

Z

Zuni tribe 80

ABOUT THE AUTHOR

Dr. Allen R. Steele worked all his life in communication media, first as a disc jockey at his college radio station, then moving up to managerial and administrative positions in international broadcasting networks. He also spent many years as a university professor in Australia and America. More recently, he has immersed himself in the history of the Southwest. Among his previous books, *Santa Fe 1880: Chronicles from the Year of the Railroad* records a most critical year in the history of Santa Fe, when rapid change overtook the old city. He now resides in the city he wrote about and enjoys sharing its incredible history with visitors on his downtown history tours.

Visit us at
www.historypress.com